*Read Two Chapters and Call Me in the Morning*

PRESCRIPTION: Laughter

Stories, Jokes, and Catastrophes Churned into Comedy

Nancy Witter

Red Penguin Books

Prescription: Laughter

Copyright © 2025 by Nancy Witter

All rights reserved.

Published by Red Penguin Books

Bellerose Village, New York

ISBN

Digital 978-1-63777-808-1

Print 978-1-63777-809-8

No part of this book may be reproduced in any form or by any electronic or mechanical means, including information storage and retrieval systems, without written permission from the author, except for the use of brief quotations in a book review.

This book is dedicated to my family, friends and all the people who taught me the lessons I needed to learn. You made me laugh, gave me content for this book and in more ways than one, saved me. To Jack, Annie and Mike, you didn't just make my life better…you made my life. Ohhh, and of course our dog… Liza Minnelli!

Annie, Jack, Me & Mike… and Liza Minnelli

Contents

Introduction	vii
1. Growing Up McDougal	1
2. We Put the Fun in Funerals	11
3. I Wanted to Be a Nun… Until I Saw Doris Day!	22
4. Wedding Hell Blues	32
5. Giddy Up Girls!	42
6. Happily Ever Laughter	55
7. Pink Slips & Punchlines	70
8. Oh Baby!	79
9. Bombs Away!	88
10. There's A Bear In My Bed!	98
11. Rain, Rome And Raphael	110
12. Spanx For The Memories	119
13. Toddlers & Tiaras Meets Medicare	130
14. I'm Not Dead Yet… But I'm Getting Closer	142
15. McDougal Motto: It Could Always be Worse	152
16. Oh Brother!	165
Epilogue	175
About the Author	181

Introduction

Well, hello there! If you're reading this, chances are someone gave it to you because they think you need a laugh or maybe you bought it yourself because you *know* you need one. Either way, welcome!

My name is Nancy Witter. For over 30 years, I've been a professional stand-up comedian, inspirational speaker, author, and NYU-certified Life Coach. Nothing makes me happier than helping people find the funny in life, especially, when times are tough. Laughter doesn't erase the struggle, but it sure makes the struggle more bearable. Sometimes, the best we can do for the people we love is offer hope and humor during their hardest moments.

In a perfect world, there would be no illness, no stress, no heartbreak, no loss. Everyone would be blissfully riding ponies, eating lollipops, and cuddling puppies. But that's not our world. Our world is messy, unpredictable, and beautifully human. And that's why we need an antidote, one that doesn't come in a bottle,

Introduction

but in the form of laughter. There's an old adage that laughter is the best medicine. I believe that's true but let's be honest, it's no replacement for your actual prescriptions. If laughter really cured everything, the pharmacy would be a comedy club.

In these pages, I share stories from every stage of my life where laughter was the medicine I needed most. From a chaotic childhood to marriage, divorce, loss, career detours, parenting, and all the other "life stuff" in between, whenever life threw a punch, I threw back a punchline! My hope is that while sharing these stories, I'll lift your spirits, give you a little laugh, and a lot of hope.

Over the years, friends, family, and even strangers have shared jokes with me. I've collected them from conversations, emails, memes, and the internet and, of course, I've written plenty of my own. Whenever one truly made me laugh, I saved it in a little file I called *The Book of Jokes.* When someone I knew was recovering from surgery, going through treatment, or simply feeling down, I'd make a personalized cover, print it out, and send it their way. My goal was simple: to give them something light, fun, and easy to read, something that could lift their spirits during chemo, a hospital stay, a heartbreak, or even just a hard day at home. This little idea was the inspiration for this book. At the end of each chapter, you'll find some of my favorite jokes from *The Book of Jokes*.

Prescription: Laughter is not only for someone who needs a lift, but also for friends and family, because sometimes it's hard to know how to cheer someone up.

Introduction

Think of this book as an alternative to flowers or a plant. It won't wilt, it doesn't need watering, and it lasts a whole lot longer. It's meant to be a hug in a book.

So sit back, relax, and let the healing begin. If you've got stitches, be careful because some of these jokes may make you laugh until you pop one. Some will make you chuckle, others might make you groan, but all are shared with love and with the hope that they give you the laugh you deserve.

Although it might seem impossible right now, one day, whatever you're going through, will just be a distant memory. Until then, remember: if you can laugh through it, you can get through it. May this book help you do just that!

With Love,
Nancy Witter

Chapter 1

Growing Up McDougal

I have always thought my ability to turn catastrophes into comedy was my superpower. I inherited this trait from my parents, Walter and Dolores McDougal. He called her Lala, and she called him Bub. They both grew up in New York, my father in Lynbrook and my mother in Brooklyn. They both spent their summers in Sayville, and that is where they met and fell in love before my dad left for the war.

Imagine the stress everyone lived with at that time, the fear of losing brothers and boyfriends, fathers and uncles. My parents had this great spirit and strength in adversity because they grew up during the depression and also had to make sacrifices and endure the hardships imposed on them from World War II. They had to laugh and keep their spirits high, for they knew that was a powerful weapon against despair. Nothing was ever that bad again in their lifetimes.

Most of my father's friends served as well. They went to war as boys and came home as men. These men and their wives then celebrated the war being over… for the rest of their lives! Everyone had house parties in those days, and they were like scenes out of Animal House. Wait until you read Chapter 15! Boy, could they drink, and they weren't a bunch of sissies like us drinking Pinot Grigio and Michelob Ultra. They had dangerous-sounding drinks like Alabama Slammers, Stingers, Martinis and Manhattans. These drinks were just made of alcohol mixed with more alcohol. They also drank Tab diet soda, which was basically battery acid in a can. They were a tough generation. It is amazing we survived!

My parents settled in Garden City, New York, a very Irish Catholic town. It wasn't unusual to have families with 7, 8, 10, or 12 kids. The Maloneys, the Murphys, the Kellys, the O'Connors, the McDougals. If you had fewer than 5 children in your family, we saw you as an only child. No wonder they drank so much.

The McDougals 1960

Parenting was very different back in the 50s and 60s. Every car came with an ashtray the size of a salad bowl, and it was always full. You could leave your baby in the

Prescription: Laughter

car while you ran into the grocery store with the windows rolled up and, my personal favorite, you could send your 7-year-old to the corner store to buy your cigarettes.

Giving birth in 1956 was ***very*** different from my giving birth in 1983. When I was studying the Lamaze Method for natural childbirth, I thought that if my mother were still alive, she would have hated this. I can just imagine trying to explain it to her. "It is a method of breathing to give pain relief without drugs during childbirth." I can hear my mother saying to me, "Nancy, if you go to a doctor and he suggests breathing as a form of anesthesia… get yourself a different doctor."

My mother and her whole generation loved to brag about how little they had to do with the birthing process. She would regale us with stories of how we came into the world. She seemed quite proud of it. She'd say, "I'd show up at the hospital, they knocked me out and I didn't see any of you until 10 days later, when I was leaving." We'd ask her, "Didn't they try to bring us to you?" She'd laugh and say, "Ohhh they tried! I told them I have a litter of kids at home… I am on vacation. I'll see the baby on the way out."

I remember one day when I was about 6, I told my mother that my teacher wanted us to bring our baby pictures to school. I was so excited when she handed me the picture, until I turned it over, and on the back it said **Steven Edward McDougal**. I said, "Mom… this is Steven's baby picture." She said, "I know, but you looked exactly like that." Then she looked at all of us and said, "You ALL looked exactly like that." One picture for everybody.

My mother was also one of those mothers who insisted that we clean our plates before we could leave the table, so eating dinner in my house was like eating at a flea market on the Lower East Side. We just bargained all through dinner. You'd hear, "I'll eat your beans if you eat my fish," or, "I'll eat your corn if you eat my potatoes." My brother Steven, whom we called the Beaver, would stand up and say, "I'll eat anyone's entire plate for five bucks." And wouldn't you know, he bought his first car with the money he made on liver night alone!

My Dad was always the life of every party and very successful. He was a lawyer for 25 years, and then he became President of Richmond Hill Savings Bank, a small savings bank in Queens, New York. He was a gifted speaker and raconteur. He was frequently invited to give speeches at golf outings, banking conferences, and fundraisers because his speeches were always littered with perfectly timed jokes that no one saw coming. I saw elegant women with long gowns, perfect make-up, and expertly coiffed hair, laughing so hard that their wine came out of their noses! People hung on his every word. It was not only rich in content but also refreshingly funny, a welcome change from the typical dry speeches. My mother was his biggest fan and greatest audience. People would love to watch her… watch him. I inherited both my love of humor and my appreciation for a well-crafted, well-delivered joke from my dad.

Prescription: Laughter

They went to Mass, and they dragged us with them. My parents had a quiet strength and a strong faith. Most of all, they loved each other, supported each other, and showed us what real, fallible, and imperfect love looks like. They made a million mistakes, but seemed to get the important stuff right. They were ethical and honest and did the hard stuff. They made all of us close because nothing brings people together like laughing at the same crazy parents.

Now for your prescribed laughter, here are some of my father's favorite jokes. These were very common type jokes in the 60's and 70's… oh, you know what else was common? Asbestos, lead paint, smoking, no seat belts, and TV dinners. Enjoy!

Nancy Witter

PRESCRIPTION: Laughter

A couple was celebrating their 50th anniversary at the Temple's Marriage Marathon. The Rabbi asked the husband, Morris, to take a few minutes and share some insight into how he managed to live with the same woman all these years. The husband replied to the audience, "Well, I treated her with respect, spent money on her, but mostly I took her traveling on special occasions." The Rabbi inquired, "Trips to where?" "For our 25th anniversary, I took her to Beijing, China." The Rabbi then said, "What a terrific example you are to all husbands, Morris. Please tell the audience what you're going to do for your wife on your 50th anniversary?" "I'm going back to go get her."

The 90-year-old man said to his doctor, "I've never felt better. I have an 18-year-old bride who is pregnant with my child. What do you think about that?" The doctor considered his question for a minute and then said, "I have an elderly friend who is a hunter and never misses a season. When he was going out in a bit of a hurry, he accidentally picked up his umbrella instead of his gun. When he got to the creek, he saw a beaver sitting beside the stream. He raised his umbrella and went *bang bang*, and the beaver dropped dead. What do you think about that?" The elderly man answered, "I'd say someone else shot the beaver." The doctor said, "My point exactly!"

———

A man walked into the produce section of his local supermarket and asked to buy half a head of lettuce. The boy working in that department told him that they only sold whole heads of lettuce. The man was insistent that the boy ask his manager about the matter. Walking into the back room, the boy said to the manager, "Some asshole wants to buy half a head of lettuce." As he finished his sentence, he turned to find the man standing right behind him, and quickly added, "And this gentleman kindly offered to *buy* the other half." The manager approved the deal, and the man went on his way. Later, the manager said to the boy, "I was impressed with the way you got yourself out of that situation earlier. We like people who think on their feet here. Where are you from, New York?" "No, Texas, sir," the boy replied. "Well, why did you leave Texas?" the manager asked. The boy said, "Sir, there's nothing but whores and football players down there." "Really?" said the manager in a tone that indicated he was insulted. "My wife is from Texas." "No kidding!" replied the boy. "Who'd she play for?"

———

A Priest and a Rabbi are sitting next to each other on an airplane. The Priest says to the Rabbi, "It's so nice to be seated next to a man of the cloth like myself. Now I understand, as a Rabbi, you could never eat pork or ham, is that right?" The Rabbi says, "Yes, that's right." The Priest then says, "Now, just between us two, have you ever had a piece of ham?" The Rabbi looked at him and whispered, "Yes, just once. It was a piece of honey-glazed Virginia ham on the bone." The Priest asked, "How did you like it?" The Rabbi exclaimed, "I loved it, and I still dream about it!" Then the Rabbi said to the Priest, "Now, I understand you as a Priest take a vow of celibacy. Is that right?" The Priest replied, "Yes, it is." Then the Rabbi said, "Well, just between us, have you ever been with a woman?" The Priest answered, "Yes, once." The Rabbi said, "How did you like it?" and the Priest shouted, "Better than ham!"

Lawyers should never ask a Mississippi grandma a question if they aren't prepared for the answer. In a trial, a Southern small-town prosecuting attorney called his first witness, an elderly woman, to the stand. He approached her and asked, "Mrs Jones, do you know me?" She responded, "Why, yes, I do know you, Mr Williams. I've known you since you were a boy, and frankly, you've been a big disappointment to me. You lie, you cheat on your wife, and you manipulate people, and talk about them behind their backs. You think you're a big shot when you haven't the brains to realize that you'll never amount to anything more than a two-bit paper pusher. Yes, I know you." The lawyer was stunned. Not knowing what else to do, he pointed across the room and asked, "Mrs Jones, do you know the defense attorney?" She replied, "Why yes, I do. I've known Mr Bradley since he was a youngster, too. He's lazy, bigoted, and he has a drinking problem. He can't build a normal relationship with anyone, and his law practice is one of the worst in the entire state. Not to mention, he cheated on his wife with three different women. One of them was your wife. Yes, I know him." The defense attorney nearly died. The judge then asked both counselors to approach the bench and, in a very quiet voice, warned, "If either of you idiots asks her if she knows me, I'll send you both to the electric chair."

———

One Saturday, a nun was in her room and started to paint it. She didn't want to get her dress and habit splattered with paint, so she decided to paint naked. She was happily painting when there was a knock on the door. She said, "Who's there?" And the man replied, "It's Nick, the blind man." She thought to herself, *What's the harm? He's blind.* She opened the door and he said "Hi, I'm Nick, and I've got your blinds."

———

An elderly man goes for his annual check up. The doctor asked him some very personal questions. "How are you sleeping?" and the patient responded, "I get 8 to 10 hours of uninterrupted sleep every night." The doctor said, "Well that's terrific!" Next, he asked, "How is your appetite?" The patient said, "Doc, I eat like a horse!" and again the doctor exclaimed, "That's just wonderful." Then the doctor asked, "Now, how are your bowel movements?" And he said, "Doc, you could set Big Ben by my regularity. Every single morning precisely at 7 o'clock, I do a long stream number 1, and a very healthy number 2." The doctor was so impressed he said, "Now that is just fantastic!" Then the patient looked at the doctor and said, "Well, it's not that fantastic… I don't get up till 9 o'clock."

———

A 75-year-old man is walking in the woods. He sees a frog, picks it up, and puts it in his pocket. The frog then begins to speak and says, "I'm not really a frog. I'm a beautiful woman, just kiss me and you'll see." The man keeps walking. She then says, "I'm also a nymphomaniac and ageless, so I'll love you literally every day for the rest of your life." The man keeps walking. She finally says, "Can you hear me?" He says, "I hear you, but at my age, I'd rather have a talking frog."

Chapter 2

We Put the Fun in Funerals

My mom and my dad were married for 25 years, and if they were alive today, they would be amazed by their 18 grandchildren and 20 great-grandchildren. Unfortunately, my mother wasn't here long, but she taught us everything we needed to know in the short 49 years she was with us.

My mother had two brothers and four sisters, and was very close to all of them and she wanted us to be close, too. She would often say to us, "You are very lucky to have each other." I always say the greatest gift she gave me was my six siblings. When you grow up in a big, chaotic family, your brothers and sisters become your comrades-in-arms. We all had to navigate the land mines and incoming challenges that come with a large family. It is also what brought us so close. When we get together as adults now, we rehash the old stories from our childhood and just laugh. We know it wasn't all just fun times, but that's all we remember, because it's all we focused on.

My mother was very popular. She had wonderful friends and a robust social life. She and her friends loved going to lunch, giving parties, shopping, and going to wakes. She would come home from a wake and regale my sister and I with what the deceased looked like. I remember her saying, "Peggy never looked better. I always told her she should wear some make-up and nail polish, but she never would. Thankfully, the mortician knew what to do, and she never looked better." A few weeks later, she went to another wake and came home and told my sister and me, "Poor Mary. They did a terrible job. She looks so dead." I replied, "Well, she is dead," and she said, "That's no excuse. I don't want to take any chances when I die. I don't know if I'll get someone who will do a great job like they did on Peggy, or the guy who made up poor Mary. So I made up my mind. I am going to have a closed casket and have a portrait done, so when I die, I don't have to worry if I get a good mortician or not. The last thing I want is for people to talk behind my back about how terrible I look when I'm dead." I said, "You mean like you're doing now?" And she said, "Exactly!" It reminded me of Yogi Berra when he said, "Always go to other people's funerals, otherwise they won't come to yours." She did have that portrait done, but when she died, we never used it. It didn't portray her fun spirit and sweet soul. So we chose one of her on the back of a boat, going across the Great South Bay in Sayville, NY… her happy place!

Prescription: Laughter

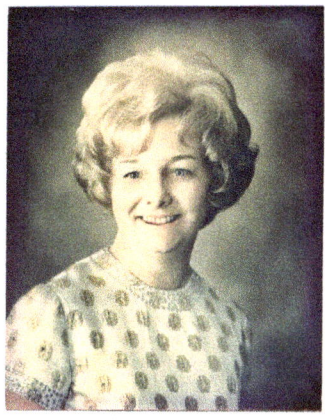

This is the portrait she wanted

This was the one we used

She had a very unusual attitude about death. I think because, especially during the war, she was subjected to a lot of death. One day, we were all at the kitchen table having dinner, and somehow the subject of death came up. I was around 11, and I remember saying to her, "Mom, if you ever die, I will never stop crying." She said, "Oh, of course you will, you'd all be fine. When Pops died (her father), we had a big party, good friends, cold beers, and a lot of laughs. We just talked about him and reminisced about the good days, just the way he would have wanted. He would have loved to have been there himself. Too bad he was dead."

In August 1972, my mother was diagnosed with cancer. My father and she had planned a trip to California to celebrate their 25th wedding anniversary. After the stage four diagnosis, my dad didn't think she should make the trip, but my mom insisted. She had never been to California, and she also didn't want to disappoint my father. So off they went. They left in late October and when they got home in early November, she was very sick, and died just a few weeks later on December 5, 1972. I was 15, my youngest sister Peanut, was 14, and the oldest was 24. We had a two day wake and the place was packed day and night. It was just the way she would have wanted it. People were sad, of course, but we were raised to put our grief aside so that other people wouldn't feel bad for us.

Her wake was a very social event, very typical for my family, and then after the funeral, we all went back to my house. It was overflowing with people drinking, eating, crying, and laughing. Later in the day my dad started entertaining everyone. He recited her favorite poems that he would often perform, *Casey At The Bat* and *The Cremation of Sam McGee*, along with joke after joke just as if she were still there laughing harder than anybody.

At my house, one of my girlfriends said to me, "Are you going to celebrate Christmas this year?" and I said, "I think so, why?" She responded, "Because your mother just died" and I said "Yeah... I don't think that's

Prescription: Laughter

going to stop us from celebrating Christmas." And it didn't. My father decided at the last minute to have a huge Christmas party on Christmas Eve. He went to all the neighbors and personally invited them on December 23rd, the rest of his friends he called. My Aunt Rose and Uncle Jerry came in on Christmas Eve in the middle of the party like Santa Claus. They came with bags and bags and bags full of gifts for us. My father had given my Aunt Rose his credit card and told her to do the Christmas shopping and she did a fantastic job. She knew how to spend my father's money just like my mother did. We got the best stuff ever that year!

Well, Christmas songs were playing and drinks were flowing and conversations were carrying on. I walked down the hallway, and I was behind one of our new neighbors who we didn't know very well and I heard him say to his wife, "Didn't the mother just die?" And she just said, "Yes… but you know the Irish." Then at midnight my sister Carol got engaged. Her ring, which had been my mother's engagement ring, was hanging from the Christmas tree. Now we had another reason to celebrate besides Christmas. I'm sure a psychologist could have written volumes about this, but we knew our mother wouldn't want it any other way. She would have loved it.

In times of tragedy and sadness if you look hard enough, you'll find the diamond in the rough, and the silver lining in the cloud. Grieving, of course is healthy and necessary, but it is not a place that we can live in for a very long period of time before it begins to whittle away at your spirit. So we honored her by loving and taking care of each other. When we talk about my mother, we remember what a character she was, how she loved to decorate, host parties, and have the biggest Thanksgiving usually with 30+ of our favorite aunts, uncles and cousins. How she would laugh at my father's jokes and her quiet strength in the face of overwhelming adversity. There is a great quote that I love that says "God gave us memories so that we might have roses in December." Every December I remember to thank my mother for all the roses she gave me.

They often talk about an Irish goodbye or Irish exit. That is when you don't say goodbye, rather you silently exit the party or gathering without saying goodbye to anyone. Then there is the other Irish goodbye. That's when you say goodbye and you never leave! Now that's the kind of goodbye my family uses because we hate to say goodbye. So we just say so long… see you soon, and we know we will.

The Irish always enjoy a good story and great jokes, so here is my prescription of laughter. Enjoy these drop-dead funny jokes!

PRESCRIPTION: Laughter

Patrick O'Connor was lonely, and so he decided life would be more fun if he had a pet. So he went to the pet store and told the owner that he wanted to buy an unusual pet. After some discussion, he finally bought a centipede (100-legged bug), which came in a little white box to use for his house. He took the box back home, found a good location for the box, and decided he would start off by taking his new pet to the local pub to have a drink. So he asked the centipede in the box, "Say Lad, would you like to go to O'Neil's with me for a pint?" But there was no answer from his new pet. This bothered him a bit, but he waited a few minutes and then asked him again, "Say Lad as I said I just want to know if you want to go to O'Neil's with me for a pint?" But again, there was no answer from his new friend and pet. So he waited a few minutes more, thinking about the situation. He decided to ask him one more time, this time putting his face up against the centipede's house and shouting, "Now, Lad, this is the last time I'm asking. I said, 'Would you like to go to O'Neil's and have a pint with me?'" Finally, a little voice came out of the box and it said, "I heard you the first time! Give me a minute. I'm putting on my fecking shoes!!!"

Nancy Witter

———

There once were two Irishmen, named Shawn and Paddy, who were the best of friends. During one particular night of revelry, the two agreed that when one passed on, the other would take and spill the contents of a bottle of fine, Irish whiskey over the grave of the fondly missed and recently dead friend. And as fate would have it, Shawn would be the first to pass. Paddy, hearing of his friend's illness, came to visit his dear friend one last time. "Shawn?" said Paddy. "Can you hear me?" Faintly, Shawn replied, "Yes, Paddy, I can." Paddy started, "Do you remember our pact, Shawn?" "Yes, I do Paddy" Then Paddy said, "And you'll also remember that I was to pour the contents of a fine, old bottle of whiskey over your grave, which we have been saving for, going on 30 years now." "Yes, Paddy, I do," whispered Shawn. "It's a very old bottle now, you know?" urged Paddy. Then, with all the force he could muster Shawn said, "What the hell are you gettin' at Paddy?" So he whispered, "Well, Shawn, when I pour the whiskey over your grave… Would ya mind if I filter it through my kidneys first?"

———

Patrick O'Connor hoisted his beer and said, "Here's to spending the rest of me life in between the legs of me wife!" That won him the top prize at the pub for the best toast of the night! He then went home and told his wife, Mary, "I won the prize for the best toast of the night." She said, "Aye, did ye now. Ya big fool, what did you say in your toast?" Patrick said, "I got up in front of the Lads and I said here's to spending the rest of me life, sitting in church beside me wife." "Oh, that is very nice indeed, Patrick!" Mary said. The next day, Mary ran into one of Patrick's drinking buddies on the street corner. The man chuckled leeringly and said, "Ya know Mary, Patrick won the prize the other night at the pub with a toast about you." She said, "Aye, he told me, and I was a bit surprised, because he's only been there twice, and both times I had to pull him by the ears just to get him to come."

―――

Father O'Malley answers the phone.
"Hello, is this Father O'Malley?"
"It is."
"This is the IRS. Can you help us?"
"I can."
"Do you know a Bobby Lynch?"
"I do."
"Is he a member of your congregation?"
"He is."
"Did he donate $10,000 to the church?"
"He will."

―――

An Irish daughter had not been home for over five years. Upon her return, her father cussed her. "Where have ye been all this time? Why did you not write to us, not even a line? Why didn't you call? Can you not understand what you put yer old Mum thru?" The girl, crying, replied, "Dad....sniff, sniff...I became a prostitute." "You what!!?" Then her Dad screamed, "Get out of here, you shameless harlot! Sinner! You're a disgrace to this family." She looked at her Dad and said "OK, as you wish. I just came back to give Mum this luxurious fur coat, title deed to a ten-bedroom mansion plus a savings certificate for $5 million. For my little brother, this gold Rolex and for you Daddy, the sparkling new Mercedes limited edition convertible that's parked outside plus a membership to the country club ... (takes a breath) and an invitation for you all to spend New Year's Eve on board my new yacht in the Riviera." The father said "Now what was it you said you had become?" The daughter, crying again, "A prostitute Dad! Sniff, sniff." Then her Dad said, "Oh Bejesus! Ye scared me half to death, girl! I thought ye said a Protestant. Come here and give your old man a hug!"

A man stumbles up to the only other patron in a local bar and asks if he can buy him a drink. "Why, of course," the man replies in a thick Irish accent. "Where are you from?" asks the first man. "County Clare!" replies the second. "Really?" says the first man. "Aye'm from County Clare too! Bartender, put up two pints for County Clare!" The two of them drink to the County of Clare. "So where in Clare are ye from?" asks the first man. "Doolin." replies the second. "Did ye hear that, Joe?" says the first man. "Aye'm from Doolin too! Put up another round - for Doolin!" The two men drink to Doolin. "So where did ye go to school?" asks the first. "St. Mary's," answers the second. "St. Mary's, really? Noooo! AYE went to St. Mary's too! Bartender, another round for St. Mary's!" They guzzle it down. A regular patron has just sat down at the bar, and says to Joe the bartender, "So Joe, what is going on over there?" The bartender says, "Oh, nothing much. The O'Connor twins are just drunk again."

Chapter 3

I Wanted to Be a Nun... Until I Saw Doris Day!

I was always a very impressionable kid. I loved movies and drama and that eventually inspired me to go to the American Academy of Dramatic Arts in New York City. I saw everything through the lens of a movie. My first career choice in second grade was to be a nun, because I loved the outfit. My favorite nun was Sister Antonio Maria. She wore a floor length navy blue dress and had a long flowing habit on her head. When I would wrap a towel around my head, or I took a sweater off, I would push it back to the beginning of my hairline and let it dangle down my back and pretend I was her. I also loved the movie, *The Bells of Saint Mary's* with Ingrid Bergman. I thought to myself, *That's what I wanna be. They're so good and so beautiful.*

When I was 9, I saw the movie, *The Song of Bernadette*, starring Jennifer Jones, and was inspired. One day while my mother was out to lunch with her friends, I thought I would surprise her and wash the kitchen floor. The only reason I did that was because Bernadette had done it in

Prescription: Laughter

the movie. Jennifer Jones had a kerchief on her head, so I made sure I put one on as I scrubbed the floor. I was so dramatic, that as I was scrubbing the floor, I was quietly hoping that the Blessed Virgin Mary would look down on me and think I was a saint, too.

A few years later, when I was making my confirmation, I needed to pick a saint's name. I picked Bernadette as my name just because I liked Jennifer Jones so much. My friend Danny McWilliams is a very talented comedian and his confirmation joke was, "The nun said to me 'Mr. McWilliams in order to make your confirmation you have to pick a saint's name.' So I picked Eva Marie." Eva Marie **Saint,** for those of you who are not familiar, was a very popular actress in the 50's and 60's… hence the joke.

The obsession with being a nun wore off quickly. I left Saint Anne's school and spent the third grade in public school. I remember the day our teacher asked everyone in the class, what famous person they would like to be. Some people said Martha Washington, some said Abraham Lincoln, or Florence Nightingale. I said I wanted to be Doris Day.

Why? Because she was beautiful, she could sing and

Rock Hudson was always her love interest. So much better than wearing a habit! I never realized what a shallow kid I was.

By the time I got to junior high, I volunteered as a Candy Striper in a hospital and I worked with a woman who was in an iron lung because she had contracted polio. I wrote letters for her, gave her water to drink and kept her company. I went twice a week. One of the reasons I volunteered as a Candy Striper was because I liked the outfit. It was adorable.

That was where I saw first hand all that the nurses did and I became obsessed with them. I thought nurses were heroes and I still do. In the movies, the nurses were always pretty and the men, usually soldiers, always seemed to be so grateful for everything they did. They were just so good, smart and brave. Also… you guessed it, I loved the cute outfit. The white hat and white dress, and the navy blue cape like in *Call The Midwife* are to die for.

Prescription: Laughter

When my mother got sick, I got a book called, *The Art of Practical Nursing*. I was 15 and I read everything I could about how to care for someone with cancer, and that was when I decided I was going to attend nursing school. I wanted to pursue my studies at Marymount University in Virginia, because they had a great nursing program. I had it all planned out, except for the fact that I was terrible in math, biology, chemistry and a terrible student overall. I was voted *class clown*, and as my father used to joke, I graduated Summa Cum Lucky from high school. I remember a teacher said to the class, "Can anyone name a book that made them cry?" I emphatically replied, "Algebra!"

I hated math. It was my least favorite subject. In fact, there was a class the administrators implemented because they realized there was a small group of students who couldn't do algebra, geometry, trigonometry or calculus. These were the people that were going to have to learn to make change for the rest of their lives and they called it Business Math. My friend Jack Foley sat next to me and we had a pop-up quiz one day. The first question was "Someone comes into your store and buys something for $7 and they hand you a $20 bill. How much change do you give them?" I leaned over to Jack and said "Can I cheat off of you?" He said, "It's $13." I shouted back, "I don't have that kind of money, Jack!"

So nursing school was out. Plan B (it meant something different in 1975) for me was to audition for the American Academy of Dramatic Arts in New York City. Miracle of miracles, I got in. I didn't end up going immediately, but I did attend night school there two years later, when I got my first job in New York City.

Years later, when my dad was dying due to congestive heart failure and diabetes and needed hospice, I was appointed his health care advocate. I wanted to run out and get a white hat and blue cape, but they didn't sell them anymore…awww shucks! The nurses came for a few hours every day and were lifesavers in every way. They were a comfort to my family, a champion for my father, and made this very difficult time so much easier to bear, because we knew he was in the best of hands. Those nurses guided us every bit of the way. They were miracle workers, angels on earth, along with the social workers, who were a tremendous help as well. Come to think of it, they should all wear capes because they are true superheroes.

One incident stands out from that time. I was asking my father details about his life, partially because I wanted to know some of them before he passed on, and secondly, it would be helpful for his obituary. I never let on that it was one of the reasons I was asking. So, he

Prescription: Laughter

started telling me about the details of his life and then he said "Now Nan…make sure you put all of that in the obituary and while you're at it mention that I was a very funny, charming and handsome guy." I assured him that I would never leave that part out.

He wasn't afraid of death, in fact, he was ready. He always said, "there are way worse things than death." I then remembered that he had been a witness to World War II. A few days later, he was near the end, and my sisters and I surrounded his bed as we helped lift him up by the sheets to reposition him so he would be more comfortable. He always loved Mallowmars and chocolate pudding, anything sweet really, but because of his diabetes they were forbidden foods. Now, there was no sense in denying him whatever he wanted. So while we surrounded his bed we were feeding him Mallomars, chocolate covered graham crackers, and chocolate pudding. He looked up at us with a big smile on his face, and he said, "You know dying is kind of fun. I never knew that before, because I never died before." It broke the tension and gave us a wonderful memory of him, one that we carry with us, all these years later. He died on May 10th, 2001.

Now if you can't have a mallomar, or chocolate pudding, to feel better take my prescription for laughter, it's sweet without sugar!

Nancy Witter

PRESCRIPTION: *Laughter*

A woman went to the doctor's office where she was seen by one of the Nurse Practitioners. After about four minutes in the examination room, she burst out screaming as she ran down the hall. An older doctor stopped her and asked what the problem was and she told him her story. After listening, he had her sit down and relax in another room. The older doctor marched down the hallway to where the Nurse Practitioner was writing in her chart. "What's the matter with you?" the older doctor demanded. "Mrs. Reid is 62 years old, has four grown children and seven grandchildren and you just told her she was pregnant?" The Nurse Practitioner continued writing and without looking up said, "Does she still have the hiccups?"

———

A patient sees a nurse and says, "Nurse, I keep seeing spots in front of my eyes." The nurse replies, "Have you seen a doctor?" He said, "No, just the spots."

———

Prescription: Laughter

A nurse walks into the doctor's office and says, "There's an invisible man in the waiting room." The doctor replies, "Tell him I can't see him right now."

———

A gorgeous young redhead goes into the doctor's office and says that her body hurts wherever she touches it. "Impossible!" says the doctor. "Show me." The redhead took her finger, pushed on her left breast and screamed and then she pushed her elbow and screamed even more. She pushed her knee and screamed and likewise she pushed her ankle and screamed. Everywhere she touched made her scream. The doctor said, "You're not really a redhead, are you?" "Well, no," she said. "I'm actually a blonde." "I thought so," replied the doctor. "Your finger is broken."

———

Two men are convicted of murder and receive the death penalty. The judge asks them if they have any last requests. The first man says, "I'd like to hear Billy Ray Cyrus sing 'My Achy, Breaky Heart.'" The judge says, "Done." Then the judge says to the other man, "Now sir, what is your last request?" and he says, "I'm begging you… kill me first!"

———

A young couple has their first child. Their joy slowly turns to concern, however, when for three years the child never utters a word. They hired speech therapists, doctors and psychiatrists, but the boy simply refused to speak. Then one morning when the child was five, he looked up from his breakfast and said, "My oatmeal's cold." The couple is stunned. The father finally speaks. "Son," he says, "Why have you waited so long to say something?" The kid shrugs, "Up until now, there was nothing to complain about."

Teacher: "If you had one dollar and you asked your father for another, how many dollars would you have?" Johnny: "One dollar." Teacher: "You don't know your arithmetic." Johnny: "And you don't know my father!"

A delivery driver knocks on a door, and a little kid holding a beer and puffing on a cigar answers. The driver asks, "Are your parents home?" The kid takes the cigar out of his mouth and says, "What the hell do you think?"

Recently, a large hospital hired several cannibals to increase their diversity. "You are all part of our team now," said the Human Resources rep during the

Prescription: Laughter

welcoming briefing. "You get all the usual benefits and you can go to the cafeteria for something to eat, but please don't eat any employees." The cannibals promised they would not. Four weeks later their boss remarked, "You're all working very hard and we have noticed a marked increase in the performance of our employees. However, one of our nurses has disappeared. Do any of you know what happened to her?" The cannibals all shook their heads, "No." After the boss had left, the leader of the cannibals said to the others, "Which one of you idiots ate the nurse?" A hand rose hesitantly. "You fool!" the leader continued. "For four weeks we've been eating managers and doctors and no one noticed anything. But now, you had to go and eat someone who actually does something."

Chapter 4

Wedding Hell Blues

I love a good "and they lived happily ever after" ending, especially, when the people I love are married, and stay that way. It doesn't always happen, but I'm so happy when it does. When I was young I loved attending weddings. It was a chance to dress up, and watch the bride glide down the aisle on the arm of her father. I loved the reception, the free drinks, the dancing, the loud bands, the touching moments when the groom danced with his bride for the first time, and the much anticipated father-daughter dance. It was all so emotional, exciting, always filled with real drama. Every single girl would think, *I hope one day, that will be me.* That is where the expression, "Be careful what you wish for," was born.

Then there came a time when I noticed a shift about how my father felt about going to weddings. He started saying, "I'm not going to the church, I'll just go to the reception." I was shocked. "But the wedding is the best

Prescription: Laughter

part!" By the time he got older, my father flat-out hated weddings. I thought to myself, *How is that possible?*

Then when I was in my 30's, my dislike came from a different angle: the dreaded morning after brunch. One day, after a wedding, way back in the '80's, my Aunt Mary squinted at me as I walked into the brunch and asked, "And how are YOU feeling this morning?" I answered, "Great, why?" She smirked, "You fell on the dance floor last night." I snapped, "My heel broke!" Then my sister-in-law chimed in, "And you were making out with the busboy." I said, "So? I liked him. We had a lot in common." She raised an eyebrow and said, "Really? He didn't even speak English." I shot back, "I'm bilingual… you don't know everything about me!" I always had to defend my bad decisions, which led me to believe that I would make a great defense attorney. In most instances, I would have hired myself. I wanted to go back to the reception hall in the hotel and ask where their Lost and Found was, and when they'd ask me what I had lost I'd say, "My dignity."

Now I'm 68 and I totally get why my father hated weddings. I get an invitation to a wedding and all I can think is "Oh boy, this is going to cost a fortune!" When it's a destination wedding it's even worse. I'd rather pick my own destination if I'm going to go away, and I'd rather pay for my own meals, and booze. I'd be just as happy seeing the wedding highlights on Instagram and sending a gift from Amazon.

When the wedding is too big, you wait in line forever for a drink and can never find the people you want to find. Too small, and you're forced into awkward small talk with people you'll never see again. The whole episode is exhausting. Then the band starts and now no one can hear anything anybody is saying, your feet hurt, and your Spanx are starting to cut off the circulation below your waist. There are some weddings that are more memorable than others, but, the truth is, the best weddings are nice but forgettable. It's the disasters you remember forever.

The best disastrous wedding was when my cousin Patty got married in the early '80s. The ceremony and reception were held on a party boat that, up until then, had only ever been used as a fishing charter. In fact, Patty's wedding was the boat's very first event as a private party charter. We left from the South Street Seaport in New York City. We were going to go around the Statue of Liberty, where the couple would recite their vows, and then return directly after sunset.

As soon as the boat left the dock, I was the first one in line to get a drink. I asked for a beer as it was 98° on a hot August day. The bartender then told me they didn't have any beer. I said to him, "As far as I can see there are nothing but O'Neils, McDougals and Gleasons, and you are the one who has to tell them there is no beer on this boat. Good luck to you. I'd rather tell Hilter that he was losing the war." As an afterthought I added, "You're about to have a very bad day!"

Meanwhile, Billy Joel and Christie Brinkley were also getting married in the harbor that day, and we were hoping someone on our boat would get drunk enough to jump overboard, swim over and beg them for beer.

So we did the next best thing. We either had vodka tonics or gin and tonics and other variations of a cold drink, over ice in a plastic cup. Then they started to run out of stuff. First it was the ice, and then booze, and then the plastic cups. They had put out some version of a charcuterie board in the blazing sun, which we ended up throwing in the harbor as shark chum because we didn't want to get food poisoning. Then they brought out a three-tier wedding cake. They left that in the sun and as the bride went to cut it, the layers started sliding off each other.

As the boat rocked on, mascara melted, hair flattened, and the men stripped off ties and jackets. My father kept the morale afloat with a steady stream of jokes until, at last, we docked. And then…salvation! At the end of the pier stood a hot dog truck, gleaming like an oasis, with ice-cold sodas. Within seconds, we were sprinting like Usain Bolt, desperate to guzzle a drink and dump ice over our overheated heads.

Then a bunch of us went for a drink at this lovely

bar by the South Street Seaport, and I was doubled over laughing with my sisters and cousins about the disastrous but hilarious day. When my cousin Patty, the bride, leaned over and asked me, "Nancy, was it really that bad?" I looked at her and said, "Patty, it was so bad… it was great. If it had been just a little less bad, it would've just been a sad wedding that we'd barely remember. But this? This is a wedding that will live in infamy. I'm calling it the Death Boat because we all cheated death today! Now who's going to forget that?"

Well, she actually sued the boat company and won, and a few years later she got divorced. The marriage didn't last, but the memory of that day still does. That wedding on that boat taught me something. If you make up your mind to have a good time despite the circumstances, you will. All it takes is a little reframing turning "terrible" into "terribly funny."

It's been more than 45 years, and whenever my cousins and I get together and this story comes up, we laugh until we cry. Every hilarious, disastrous detail is still as fresh now as it was that night. And you know what? That's not just a wedding… that's a great wedding!

There is a happy bonding that happens when things go off the rails. Everyone is suddenly "in it together" with a sense of "We'll always have that." A shared disaster becomes an anchor memory. It's not just a wedding or a dinner party, it's the wedding where the best man fainted or the dinner where the dog ate the roast. These are the stories that become family lore. So embrace them, remember them, and celebrate them!

Prescription: Laughter

Now here is your prescription to find the funny in love and marriage and the hilarity that they inspire.

Nancy Witter

PRESCRIPTION: *Laughter*

A couple is seeing a marriage counselor. He asks the wife, "What is it you need from your husband?" She replies, "I need more kisses, more hugs, more affection, more connection." With that the therapist gets up, grabs the wife, and makes out with her for a few minutes. When he's done, he puts her down on her feet and says, "That is what your wife needs three times a week." The husband looks back and says, "Well… I can drop her off on Mondays and Wednesdays but on Friday… I go fishing."

A wife was making a breakfast of fried eggs for her husband. Suddenly, her husband burst into the kitchen screaming, "Careful," he said, "CAREFUL! Put in some more butter! Oh my GOD! You're cooking too many eggs at once. IT'S TOO MANY! Turn them! TURN THEM NOW! We need more butter. Oh my GOD! WHERE are we going to get MORE BUTTER? They're going to STICK! Careful. CAREFUL! I said, be CAREFUL! You NEVER listen to me when you're cooking! Never! Turn them! Hurry up! Are you CRAZY? Have you LOST your mind? Don't forget to salt them. You know you always forget to salt them. Use the salt. USE THE SALT! THE SALT!" The wife stared at him. "What in the world is wrong with you? You think I don't know how to fry a couple of eggs?" The husband calmly replied, "I just wanted you to know what it feels like when I'm driving."

———

Joe died. His *will* provided $30,000 for an elaborate funeral. As the last guests departed, his wife, Helen, turned to her oldest friend, Jody, and said. "Well, I'm sure Joe would be pleased." Jody replied "I'm sure you're right," then she lowered her voice and leaned in close. "How much did this really cost?" "Thirty thousand?" "No!" Jody exclaimed. "I mean, it was very nice, but $30,000?" Helen answered, "The funeral was $6,500. I donated $500 to the church. The wake, food and drinks were another $500 the rest went for the memorial stone." Jody computed quickly. "$22,500 for a memorial stone? My God, how big is it?!" The widow said "2 ½ carats."

———

A husband and wife were having dinner at a very fine restaurant when this absolutely stunning young woman comes over to their table, gives the husband a big open mouthed kiss, then says "I'll see you later" and walks away with a provocative shashay in her stride. The wife glares at her husband and says, "…And who, may I ask, was that?!!" "Oh," replies the husband, "...she's my mistress." "Well, that's the last straw!" says the wife. "I've had enough of your philandering ways!! I want a divorce!" "I can understand that," replies her husband, "but remember if we get a divorce, it will mean no more of those shopping trips to Paris, no more wintering in Barbados, no more summers in Tuscany, no new Jaguar in the garage and no more yacht club membership and your fancy ladies socials. But hey, the decision is yours." Just then, a mutual married friend enters the restaurant with a gorgeous babe on his arm. "Who's that woman with Sal?" asks the wife. "That's *his* mistress," says her husband. She replied "Hmmmph! ...Ours is much prettier."

———

A 60-year-old couple were celebrating their 25th wedding anniversary and were out antiquing when they came across what looked like a genie lamp. They rubbed it as a joke but to their surprise, out pops Jeanne the genie who says, "I'm not an ordinary genie, I'm an anniversary genie, which means you each get one wish." So she looked at the wife and said, "What would you like for your anniversary?" She said, "I'd like two round-trip tickets on the Queen Mary for my husband and I," and then BAM, two tickets were in her hand. Then the genie turned to the husband and asked, "What would you like for your anniversary?" The husband said, "I'd like a wife that's 30 years younger," and BAM, just like that… he turned 90!

Prescription: Laughter

———

A young son asked, "Is it true Dad, that in some parts of Africa a man doesn't know his wife until he marries her?" Dad replied, "That happens in every country, son."

———

One day, a man came home and was greeted by his wife dressed in a very sexy nightie. She looked at him with sultry eyes and purred, "Tie me up, and you can do whatever you want." So, he tied her up and went golfing.

Chapter 5
Giddy Up Girls!

My Aunt Nancy once said, "Great friends halve your sorrows and double your joy." I have always thought that friends are not a luxury, they are a necessity. I always say, love is a verb, because it is an action word. The best way for people to know you love them is to show up. I know this because my friends and family have shown up for me my entire life.

My definition of a great friend is someone who will hate whomever I hate, in that moment when I am either hurt or infuriated… whether it is my husband, my sisters, or friends. Then when the spat is over and all has been forgiven, they will forgive them too and forget it ever happened. As one friend said, "You just tell me who you hate and I'll hate them, too." And I thought, *Oh boy, hate like that, is real love.*

Some life lessons are taught by unsuspecting teachers. Belmont Racetrack is where I learned one of my most valuable life lessons. You see, I live around the corner from Belmont Park Racetrack in Floral Park, New York. It is where the Belmont Stakes, the last leg of the Triple Crown, is run.

I love going to the racetrack because it almost feels like I am at a Broadway show. The pageantry before the race is run is beautiful and exciting. The racetrack Bugle Page plays "Call to Post," then out of a long dark tunnel into the sunlight comes the magnificent thoroughbreds. Upon them sit the small jockeys wearing their dynamic brightly colored "jockey silks."

Among all the racetrack traditions my favorite is that of the "buddy horse" or the escort horse. These are the horses that you will see walking alongside the thoroughbreds out to the starting gate. The job of the buddy horse, I was told by a veteran horse trainer, is to keep the thoroughbreds calm by keeping them company as they make their way to the gate. They also serve to give comfort and confidence to their equestrian friends. The buddy horse is happy to defer to his friend, and if he can help by keeping him calm and happy so that he can win the race, he is happy to oblige.

Now after watching several races and visiting the horses on a private tour back at the stable, I had a great revelation. I found the biggest difference between the buddy horse and thoroughbred isn't in breeding, it is in its purpose. In a race, the purpose of the thoroughbred is to win the race and the purpose of the buddy horse is to enable him to win the race. It would be a mistake for the buddy horse to compare himself to the thoroughbred or to try to run his race.

Everyone needs a buddy horse. This is the friend

that believes in you more than you believe in yourself. The person that gives you confidence, that sees the best in you in such a strong profound way that you feel inspired to take chances. With a buddy horse at your side you can find the kind of strength and courage you never knew you had. If you fail, your buddy horse will say "get back on the horse." If you succeed, your buddy will say "I told you so."

I met my oldest buddy horses in 7th grade. When I first met them I said, "Why the long faces?" (I couldn't resist!) We are still close friends to this day. I moved from Long Island to Leland, North Carolina, around five years ago and three of my friends from 50 years ago moved here, too. Sometimes I feel like I'm in an episode of the Golden Girls of Garden City, full of laughs and love. This year we attended our 50th high school reunion together.

Left to right: Nancy, Carol, Rose, and Cathy

I feel like I'm in that movie "Big" with Tom Hanks, who's a 30-year-old man in a 13-year-old body. The only difference is I'm a 68-year-old woman in a 68-year-old body, but my brain feels like I'm still 25. I think that's because for the first time in my life, I'm not living with my parents, I'm not living with my kids, I can't get pregnant and I have the key to the liquor cabinet! It's so much fun. My shopping list now looks like this…Cheese Doodles, Häagen-Dazs ice cream, and rolling papers. I'm so happy that I'm this old, I'm here with my old friends and my fabulous new friends.

When people retire, downsize and move, it's like being in your first year in middle school or high school or college. You don't know anyone and you'll have to make new friends all over again. I remember when we met our great friends Rick and Val, a few months after we moved to Leland. Their daughter, Grace, was a server at a local restaurant and had told us we should meet her parents as she thought we'd all get along great. One night, quite by accident, we did. We went up to the bar to have a drink and we found our friend Eileen talking to this nice couple. She introduced us and mid-conversation, we realized they were Grace's parents.

Meeting new friends is so weird. You feel so awkward and stupid because you don't know how to begin a friendship. It feels like an episode on Larry David or Seinfeld "Do we ask them for their numbers? Do you think they'd like to go trivia with us?" We did ask them if they wanted to go to trivia, and in turn they asked us over for dinner beforehand. From that night on we became the greatest of friends. We met their friends and they met my family and friends. We now we have a big beautiful network of fun, wonderful people to play with, along with two out of my three sisters who now live in Wilmington, too.

Rick, Grace and Valarie

Old friends are particularly special. That is because they are the only ones that knew your parents and your siblings, had been in the bedroom you grew up in, and had been at your kitchen table. They were right there beside you as you were growing up. I have this very funny memory of my dearest friend Cathy.

My father and my sister, Ditta, had a small fight on a Saturday afternoon and Ditta decided she would sleep over at her friend Donna's house. I asked Cathy if she wanted to sleep over because we could sleep in Ditta's bedroom which had twin beds. We were about 16 and Cathy said sure. We stayed up late, probably not going to bed until 1:00 a.m., just laughing and whispering like teenage girls do. Not long after, we heard my father come home. We decided to be quiet, hoping he'd think we were asleep and not want to disturb us. But, he came in anyway. He didn't even turn the light on. He just sat down on the side of Ditta's bed where Cathy was sleeping and which was right next to the door. Just for reference my sister Ditta had long blonde hair and bright blue eyes, Cathy, on the other hand, was a beautiful brunette, with brown-eyes. Now my father had had a few drinks, and began to apologize for the earlier argument. It was actually very heartfelt. He said, "I'm sorry, Ditta. I just want you to know, I think you're a home run and I want to thank you for all you do around here. I love you kiddo."

Meanwhile, I'm in the next bed, cringing under the covers, thinking, "Oh God. What's Cathy gonna do? Please, Cathy, just play dead. Pretend you're asleep." But without missing a beat, as soon as my father finished with, "I love you kiddo," Cathy calmly looked up and said, "I love you too, Daddy." He then got up, kissed her on the forehead and closed the door. That was 55 years ago and to this day, it's still one of my favorite stories. Cathy may not have been family when she walked into my house, but she sure as hell was by the time she walked out.

There was another time when I found myself struggling financially. I spent the weekend at Cathy's house. I know I must've been tense that weekend, but I never told her the financial bind I was in. She was a very successful executive and if I had asked her, I'm sure she would have lent me anything that I needed. There was just no way I was going to do that. She lived in Pennsylvania and I worked in New York City so on Monday morning, on her way to work, she dropped me at the Amtrak train station, as she did whenever I visited. As I was pulling into Penn Station, I went into my pocketbook to take out a lipstick and I found a small envelope. I couldn't imagine what it could be and when I opened it it was a simple card and it just said "Just because…" and there were ten $100 bills in there. Unbeknownst to her, that was the exact amount of money I was short. She also bought my wedding dress when I got married at 50. A kind, generous, fun friend indeed. She is my golden girl friend, and I say to her often, "I love you kiddo."

My best friend Carol did something equally beautiful for me. I was a struggling single mother. I had just started my job in New York City and for my 40th birthday she enrolled me in and paid for my first comedy class. I never would've been able to afford it on my own and I never forgot it. She believed in me, and my talent and that made all the difference. It changed my life, and was the beginning of my career in writing and performing stand-up comedy. In the past 50 years, she is the one that has made everything in my life possible. She's a thoroughbred of a person, and my buddy horse in life.

Then there is my Rose, she is a champion buddy horse. She is our official historian and recalls things we have long forgotten. She is the one that remembers who we were, before we became who we are. She's the one that makes me laugh, she shows up and always makes me feel like a superstar. . She is smart, beautiful, generous, and so thoughtful…lucky me. I am so glad we are all in the same race together.

My mother always had great buddy horses. She was a wonderful hostess and party giver, a fabulous cook and entertainer. She loved giving parties but she was not good at time management or cleaning up in the kitchen as she went along. Right before every big party her nerves would get the best of her. She'd scream at us to clean up and put our things away. We all waited with bated breath for that doorbell to ring because we knew the cavalry was coming, as it always did. You could set your watch by it. Approximately an hour before any party, my mom's friends, Betty, Millie, Mary, and Peggy would come in and take over the house. They usually arrived minutes after a full and total meltdown. So it was not unusual for them to arrive at a house filled with chaos, confusion, and hysterical children. There were also carpets in need of vacuuming, and a kitchen in need of order. We would practically weep with joy that we were rescued from my mother's insanity. She was then free to get dressed and get her make-up on. Just the thought of those wonderful, generous and loving women, still warms my heart to this day. My mother was a very lucky woman to have such supportive fun friends, and the parties were always so worth it!

But her best friend was her sister, Nancy. She would talk to her on the phone as often as she could even though she lived 40 minutes away in Eastchester, NY, which was considered a long distance call in the 50s, 60s and 70s. Both of them got in trouble from their husbands for such high telephone bills. It's one of the reasons my Aunt Nancy got a full-time job at Lord & Taylor. That way she could talk to my mother whenever she wanted because she was paying the bill. You gotta love women!

My mother never drove. She had been in a bad car accident when she was 16 and was afraid of driving. Back then, of course, there was no Uber, but we did have a local taxi limousine service. My mother befriended all the drivers, and much to my dad's great surprise, she even gave them his suits. They in turn drove her everywhere, from food shopping to Christmas shopping. She finally decided she needed to get a license, not because she wanted to drive, but so she would have the proper ID to cash checks. One summer she put on her big girl pants, mustered all her courage and enrolled in driving school. She was equally shocked and thrilled when she passed the test and got her license. Then… she never drove again.

We were very lucky and blessed that after my mother died, my Aunt Nancy would come down every Wednesday, on her day off from work, to check on us. She just wanted to make sure floors were clean, and laundry was done, and that there was food in the refrigerator.

A few months after my mother died, on one of Aunt Nancy's usual visits, I showed her that the DMV had sent my mother's renewed license. My Aunt Nancy turned to me when I gave it to her, and said, "Put your coat on, we're going to the cemetery." I said "Why?" She said, "Because your mother worked so hard to get that license. I want her to have it." I thought it was the silliest thing I ever heard of, but off we went to the cemetery. She knelt down on the cold dirt and dug a few inches and placed my mother's hard-earned license there, then covered it back up and laid down a few flowers that she'd brought. When I saw the kind of love and devotion she had for her sister, her best friend, my mother, I witnessed first hand what a priceless gift love and friendship are. Here is Aunt Nancy laughing as usual. I sure do miss her laugh, but when I see this photo… I can hear it again!

Aunt Nancy and Me

There's a quote I cherish, "I once knew a man so poor, all he had was money." I know some people that are that poor. I, on the other hand, feel like the richest girl in town when I'm in the company of my fabulous friends. So, if you have great friends, understand, you are among the wealthiest people of all.

So if you want to win a race, find your buddy horse. Let them give you support and acceptance, love and confidence. Then stand ready to give it right back to them and you'll be off to the races. My buddy horses always make me feel like a Triple Crown winner!

Now take your medicine as prescribed by me… your daily dose of laughter and oh… go ahead and share them with your buddy horse!

PRESCRIPTION: Laughter

A ventriloquist is doing a show and the dummy starts going through his usual dumb blonde jokes when a blonde woman in the 4th row stands on her chair and starts shouting, "I've heard enough of your stupid blonde jokes. What makes you think you can stereotype women that way? What does the color of a person's hair have to do with her worth as a human being? It's guys like you who keep women like me from being respected at work and in the community and from reaching our full potential as a person. All because you, and your kind continue to perpetuate discrimination against not only blondes, but women in general...and all in the name of humor!" The embarrassed ventriloquist begins to apologize, and the blonde yells, "You stay out of this mister! I'm talking to that idiot on your knee."

———

Three men were asked by a priest, "When you die, what would you want people to say to you as you lay in your coffin?" The first man said, "He was an honest and good man." The second man said, "I'd like them to look down, and say, he was a loyal friend and a great husband and father." The third man said, "I'd like them to look down at me and say, "Oh my God, he's moving!"

A man was sprawled across three entire seats in a theater. When the usher came by and noticed this, he whispered to the man, "Sorry sir, but you're only allowed one seat." The man groaned but didn't budge. The usher became impatient. "Sir," the usher said, "If you don't get up from there, I'm going to have to call the manager." Again, the man just groaned, which infuriated the usher who turned and marched briskly back up the aisle in search of his manager. In a few moments, both the usher and the manager returned, and stood over the man. Together, the two of them tried repeatedly to move him, but with no success. Finally, they summoned the police. The cop surveyed the situation briefly, "All right, buddy. What's your name?" "Sam," the man moaned. "Where ya from, Sam?" the cop asked. "The balcony."

Angry, a man sits down at a bar and orders a drink. He mutters, "These lawyers are all jerks. Sitting next to him a man says, "Hey, watch your mouth." "Why, you're a lawyer?" The man responds, "No, I'm a jerk."

"Young man," said the judge, looking sternly at Conor O'Neil. "It's alcohol, and alcohol alone, that's responsible for your present sorry state!" Then with a sigh of relief the young Conor smiled at the judge and said, "I'm so glad to hear you say that. Everybody else says it's all my fault!"

———

Patrick O'Connor goes to his local donut shop and when he walks out he runs into his friend Shamus McGee. He said, "Shamus, if you guess how many donuts I have in this bag, I will give you both of them."

———

McQuillan walked into a bar and ordered martini after martini, each time removing the olives and placing them in a jar. When the jar was filled with olives and all the drinks consumed, the Irishman started to leave. "S'cuse me," said a customer, who was puzzled over what McQuillan had done, "What was that all about?" "Nothin'," said the Irishman, "my wife just sent me out for a jar of olives!"

Chapter 6

Happily Ever Laughter

I was married to Jim Witter on April 12, 1980, and divorced by 1986. We had two children within 12 months. Annie was born in December of 1983, and Michael was born in December of 1984, separated by one day, so on one day of the year every year they are both the same age. They're known as Irish twins.

Annie & Michael, my sweet Irish Twins

In December, including baby Jesus, I had too many

birthdays, too little money, too little time and needed to buy too many gifts. So every December I had my annual nervous breakdown. That's why I love Thanksgiving. Delicious food, flowing drinks, lots of fun and all that's required is that you have a great appetite and maybe bring a pie, no gift wrapping required. Lucky for me, I love pie.

In October 1990, Jimmy remarried his new wife, Angela. I remained single for the next 20 years. Then, in January 2006, I met Jack Bella. My friend Tommy's mother died, and after the burial and several drinks at lunch, we went back to his house with a whole group of friends. Later that night, we made our way down to the Bay House. This was a bar in Point Lookout, a quiet seaside community on Long Island. It was winter and there was snow on the ground so when we walked in on a Friday night at 10:00 p.m. there were only two other people at the bar. Just as we were walking in, my friend Lisa said, "Oh Jack Bella is bartending tonight… Nancy, I never thought of him for you. He's single and a great guy!" Now here's the thing… everyone knew Jack, and Jack knew everyone. The only two strangers in that bar were Jack and me. I'd had just enough to drink to feel bold, so I strutted up to the bar, looked him straight in the eye, and blurted, "You are A Door A Bull!" Without missing a beat, Jack smiled and asked, "And what are you drinking tonight?" For some reason I said, "I'll have a Bloody Mary." I never drink Bloody Marys at night. Normally I drink Coors Light, wine, or if I'm in the mood to make really bad decisions, an Irish coffee. But

Prescription: Laughter

this was not a Bloody Mary kind of bar. They didn't have tomato juice, lemons or celery. Honestly, drinking out of their glasses would require a very strong immune system and a lot of guts. So Jack took my order, said nothing, reached down and pulled out an ice cold Coors Light in a bottle, popped the top off, and put it in front of me and says "Here's your Bloody Mary. Next bar is eight miles away." I thought it was the funniest thing I ever heard a bartender say. Later, I learned this was his style. If someone ordered frozen cocktails on a very busy Saturday night and said, "Jack, can we have three frozen Margaritas?" He'd pull out three Coors Lights, crack them open, line them up and say, "There's your three frozen Margaritas. Next bar is eight miles away." No one argued. It was that kind of place.

Well, before you know it got late, and he motioned for me to come into the "kitchen." That's where the microwave was so they could heat up Ellio's pizza at 2 o'clock in the morning. And in that kitchen, he kissed me. When we both stumbled out of the kitchen, everyone at that bar asked Jack where he and I had been, and Jack said, "Nancy was helping me do inventory." They all had a great laugh at our expense. I gave him my card, and the next morning I had an email from him. A week later we saw each other again, on Super Bowl Sunday at The Bay House. We spent the whole night with friends, and after that we kept making and breaking dates thanks to weather and scheduling conflicts. In February, I had plans to go to Tortola in the British Virgin Island with friends. At the Super Bowl party we had all invited Jack to join us in Tortola, but he didn't think he could swing it. Before I left, we managed to go to dinner, once again, with a gaggle of friends. Then we finally got some time alone and we talked until 5:00 a.m.. He told me, "I'm going to try to get to Tortola, but if I can't, I'll pick you up at the airport when you get back." I said to him "You haven't been able to get past the stop sign in town, so maybe Tortola is a bridge too far." The next day was Valentine's Day and we all left for Tortola. That night I said to my friends, "Listen, I don't expect Jack Bella to come, but if he does, I will marry him." I said that because it is a very hard place to get to. You must travel by planes, boats, automobiles and drive over a volcano.

The next day was a beautiful day on the beach. We all went to our places to shower and get ready to meet at happy hour. When I opened the door to leave, I found there was a little sticky note on the door. It said "Jack Bella called. He said he'll be on the 12 o'clock ferry to the island tomorrow. Please call him at this number." To this day, it was the biggest shock of my life. The cell service was terrible, but the owners of the hotel let me make a quick call. Jack said, "Are you sure you want me to come? I mean sometimes people say something like that and then when you say you're coming, they change their mind." I replied, "Of course I want you to come." So I always say our first date was six days in Tortola. Exactly one year later we were married on that beach, just a few steps from happy hour. That happy hour turned into a very happy life.

Prescription: Laughter

Things are very different the second time around. We actually got engaged in a doctor's office. Jack had to go to a pulmonologist and he was filling out a new patient form and it said "Who do we contact in case of an emergency?" He wrote Nancy Witter, and next to it in parentheses it said "relationship" and he wrote fiancé. He then handed me the clipboard and with a sly smile said, "Did I fill that out right?" I looked at it and said, "I know what you mean… but you wrote finance." So I was turning 50 and after 20 years of being single, I found myself engaged. I gave hope to the hopeless, to those women who thought no one could find anyone after a certain age. It was odd getting married at that age. People actually asked me if I was registered anywhere. I remember thinking, *I'm 50…I have a towel, thanks.* I wish I could have registered at a place called prescriptions and procedures because they would've had the stuff I could have used.

Jack fancied himself as quite the ladies man when we were first married. He thought whenever I spoke to him that it was a "signal" that I wanted to have sex. One night I said, "Jack, can you take out the garbage?" and he said, "I know what that means!" But by the time he got back from taking out the garbage, he totally forgot what he thought he wanted.

Our birthdays are one day apart so last year for my birthday, he bought himself a prescription of Viagra, and so for his birthday… I bought him a defibrillator. As you get older the type of gifts change. One year I bought him a blood pressure machine, compression socks, and ice packs and he was so touched that I got him the things he really wanted.

He has his own love language with me. When we first started to date, I warned him how critical my first husband was of my weight and how sensitive I was about it. He was cautious to never hurt my feelings, bring up weight, or even use the word *weight*. I'd ask him, "Does this dress make me look fat?" He knew the right answer, he also knew he didn't even have to look at me to come up with the right answer. He would automatically say, "Of course not!" When I lost weight, I said to him, "Can you tell I lost weight?" And he would say "Wow you look like you're getting taller."

I love him very much and no one makes me laugh harder. I used to think, *Oh God, please let me die first, because I would miss Jack so much*. We've been married for 18 years and now, I think it would be okay. He can go first. Not because I don't love him, because I adore him. It's just that I don't think I would miss him because I always know what he is going to say before he says it. When we

Prescription: Laughter

lived in Floral Park, New York, we lived across the street from the Post Office and yet we would always get our mail at about 4 o'clock. Now I could care less about mail. Nothing good was ever found in my mailbox. The mail usually scares me. The only thing in my mail is either a bill, ValuePack, or a traffic ticket that I wasn't expecting. I could go a month without checking the mail, but Jack checked that mail every day, as if he might find the winning lottery ticket in there. Every day he would complain that we were the last ones to get the mail. Whenever he saw the mailman he'd look at me and say, "It's 4 o'clock! Can you believe it? We're just getting our mail now, and the Post Office is across the street." So one day we went for a walk and as we turned the corner on our block, I saw the mail truck in front of our apartment. I looked at my watch and it was 4 o'clock and I thought to myself… *Oh God here we go*, and sure enough right on cue he says, "It's 4 o'clock and can you believe it? We're just getting our mail now, and the Post Office is across the street." I actually lip synced his words as he said it. So it comforts me to know that if he died before me, I would never have to wonder, *Gee, what would Jack say?* I already know! Who needs a psychic?

We have a dog now. Her name is Liza Minnelli. Jack is absolutely devoted to the dog. This past New Year's Eve I was booked at a comedy club that was about three hours away. It was two shows in the same night, so I said to Jack ,"I'm gonna give you two choices, A) You can come with me to my show on New Year's Eve, or B)… and before I could say anything more he screamed "B!"

My daughter Annie and I did that show together on New Year's Eve and Jack was so happy to be at home with the love of his life "Liza Minnelli." In his defense, she is a sweet girl. When we hired a dog trainer he asked me "What would you like for me to teach her?" I said "If you teach her how to sing Cabaret and do jazz hands, that would be fantastic." We are still working on it!

Liza Minnelli and Jack

Because we have Liza Minnelli, we now love watching the Westminster dog show on TV. We love it because we see all the different breeds. My favorite part is listening to that iconic voice of the announcer introduce all the dogs. "Now entering the ring is #58, Labrador Retriever, America's most popular breed for over three decades. Originating from Newfoundland and perfected in England, the Labrador is an exceptional retriever of game on land and in water. This breed is friendly, outgoing in nature, eager to please, intelligent, and easy to train, making them exceptional family pets as well as guide or therapy dogs. #58, Labrador Retriever."

Now I watched that show this year and the thought occurred to me. *Why couldn't they have something like that for meeting men?* I mean, you then could know exactly what you're gonna get. It would've been so helpful before I married Jack. I can hear the announcer saying:

"And now entering the ring is # 81, Jack Bella. A rare breed, known for his impressive size and love of food. He can often be spotted in his natural habitat on the couch, remote in hand, watching football, baseball and basketball. He loves watching balls. His hobbies are napping, eating and drinking. His favorite food is more. This is #81 Jack Bella." I would have picked him out of the pack in a minute!

We love being retired in a place where time has no value. It feels so free that I said to him, "Do you realize we can do whatever we want, whenever we want, wherever we want?" But usually he just wants to watch reruns of Law and Order and take a nap. I'm old enough now that I'm perfectly fine with that.

I never thought I would ever get remarried. And I was perfectly content and resigned to that fact. It just goes to show you that life can change on a dime. I was a single mom for 20 years, and there were so many times I thought the stress would never end: too little money, too many bills, not enough sleep, and not enough hope. My mantra became: "By this time next year, this won't be a problem." Then I'd pray that next year would be tomorrow. When I shared my latest disaster with friends, it always sounded so ridiculously bad that we'd end up laughing, and suddenly it didn't seem quite as bad. That's how I coped. Those years of raising kids alone, on a shoestring budget was true stress. I felt inadequate as a mother, and provider. I would then make fun of myself and my circumstances knowing, "this too will pass." Now something worse might come after it, and usually it did, but I learned to process one crisis at a time. The thought that this problem won't be here forever gave me great comfort. I would take my worries and spin a funny take on it, bring it with me on stage and all of sudden it wasn't a catastrophe, it was comedy! I controlled the narrative. The problem was the same, but now I had some power over it. I always had hope that things would get better and they did. My comedy saved me. I made the greatest life-long friends, ones that understood and loved me, made me laugh hard and often. I won awards, all by making fun of things in life that went wrong. Having hope and always looking ahead to better days is what saved me… Jack's love did too.

A hopeful attitude sparks motivation and you're more likely to take proactive steps instead of giving up. Even more, hope is contagious. When you remain hopeful, you uplift others around you, creating stronger teamwork, deeper support, and a sense of shared purpose.

As Hal Lindsey said: *"Man can live about forty days without food, about three days without water, about eight minutes without air…but only one second without hope."*

Hope and laughter are just as necessary to our well-being as antibiotics. My theme song during those days was the song *High Hopes* by Frank Sinatra. If you're ever feeling a little hopeless give it a listen.

Here's your dose of laughter, prescribed to make you laugh and feel more hopeful!

Nancy Witter

PRESCRIPTION: Laughter

A cop pulls a man over in his car and says, "Are you drunk?" The man says, "No.. why?" The cop says, "Because your wife fell out of the car about five miles back!" The man says, "Oh thank God … thought I was going deaf!"

An elderly woman walked into her Senior Citizens meeting and held her clenched fist in the air and announced, "Anyone who can guess what's in my hand can have sex with me tonight!" An elderly gentleman in the back laughed and said, "Is it an elephant?" She thought about it for a minute and said… "Close enough!"

Bob, a 70-year-old, extremely wealthy widower, shows up at the Country Club with a breathtakingly beautiful and very sexy 25-year-old blonde. She hangs onto Bob's arm and listens intently to his every word. At the very first chance, Bob's friends corner him and ask, "Bob, how did you get the trophy girlfriend?" Bob replies,

Prescription: Laughter

"Girlfriend? She's my wife!" They're amazed, but continue to ask, "So, how did you persuade her to marry you?" "I lied about my age," Bob replied. "What, did you tell her? Did you tell her you were 60?" He said "No… I told her I was 90!"

———

An elderly man walks into a confessional. He says to the priest, "I am 92-years-old, have a wonderful wife of 70 years, many children, grandchildren, and great grandchildren. Yesterday, I picked up two college girls hitchhiking. We went to a motel, where I had sex with each of them three times." The priest asked, "Are you sorry for your sins?" The man says, "What sins?" The priest was horrified and asked, "What kind of a Catholic are you?" The man says, "I'm not Catholic, I'm Jewish." So the priest said: "Well then why are you telling me this?" The man says, "Father … I'm telling everybody!"

———

A man is talking to a friend and says, "We went to a great restaurant last week." And the friend says, "What is the restaurant's name?" And the guy says, "Name a flower." The friend says, "Tulip?" He replies, "No, not Tulip." He says, "Daisy?" "No, it's not Daisy." The friend then says, "Rose." The man screams in delight, "Yes, Rose!" Then slowly turns his head toward the kitchen and asks his wife, "Rose, what was that great restaurant we went to last week?"

Nancy Witter

———

The Bishop goes and sees Father O'Malley. He says, "Father O'Malley, I need you to go to Alaska. I know you'll miss the Irish countryside, but that's where you must go." Father O'Malley is not happy about it, but he agrees and he goes to Alaska. About a year later the Bishop thinks to himself, *I stuck O'Malley up there in Alaska. I should really go check on him.* The Bishop has his assistant make him a reservation and he goes to Alaska. When he gets there, the Bishop says, "So, how is it here, Father O'Malley?" O'Malley responds, "'I have to be honest with you, Bishop. It's awful, it's cold, it's dark and very few people come to Mass. As a matter of fact, if it hadn't been for my rosary and martinis, I don't think I would've lasted." He continued, "Speaking of martinis, would you like one?" The Bishop said, "You know, I think I would." Father O'Malley then turned and yelled, "Rosary, get the Bishop a martini."

———

A married Irishman went into the confessional and said to his priest, "I almost had an affair with another woman." The priest said, "What do you mean, almost?" The Irishman said, "Well, we got undressed and rubbed together, but then I stopped." The priest said, "Rubbing together is the same as putting it in. You're not to see that woman again. For your penance, say five Hail Marys and put $50 in the poor box." The Irishman left the confessional, said his prayers, and then walked over to the poor box. He paused for a moment and then started to leave. The priest, who was watching, quickly ran over to him and said, "I saw that. You didn't put any money in the poor box!" The Irishman replied, "Yeah, but I rubbed the $50 on the box, and you said it yourself, Father, rubbing is the same as putting it in!"

———

A man is born with no arms, but he grows up and starts to look for a job. He sees an ad in the paper to be a bell ringer at the local church. He visits the priest to apply for the job. The priest looks at him and says, "I wish I could help you, but I don't see how you could possibly ring our bell." The man says, "Just take me to your bell tower and I'll show you." So the priest does. The man then runs as fast as he can and slams his face against the bell, and it rings loud and clear. The priest is so impressed that he gives him the job.

Everything is going well for about six months, until one day the man takes off running to hit his face against the bell, but he overshoots and goes out the window, crashing ten stories below. A man rushes to him and holds him in his arms, waiting for the ambulance to arrive, and a woman looking on says, "OMG, who is that?" The gentleman holding him says, "I don't know, but his face rings a bell."

Chapter 7
Pink Slips & Punchlines

Life is always full of surprises, some better than others. In 2008 I was remarried, had benefits and I wanted my "to go" package from the bank where I worked. I was thrilled when they called me into the big office, though not everyone else in my department was as thrilled as I was. This was during the financial crisis in 2008. They sat me down, thanked me for the times that I entertained at some corporate events, and told me that it was very unfortunate, but my department was being eliminated and so was I. They had Kleenex on the desk which many people took advantage of. I just looked at them and said, "What took you so long? I would've fired me 10 years ago."

We all had a huge laugh, not because it was all that funny, but because those executives had to give so many people devastating news, that a little comic relief was what they needed. I was so happy because my time there was done. I was now ready to move on. You see, I was not an ideal employee. I showed up for work so infrequently that when I *did* show up, my boss greeted me like I was a guest at a cocktail party. "Hi Nancy, how are you? So good to see you! Thanks so much for coming… look, everybody… it's Nancy!" At one of my annual performance reviews, my boss said to me, "Nancy, I think you're very funny, but to be honest, I just don't think you're cut out for office work. Quite frankly, I don't know why someone as talented as you would even want a job in an office." I said, "Well… it's an ideal place to make personal phone calls and get free school supplies for the kids." I think he thought that I would agree with him and think, *He's right! I'm too good for a boring office job*. and then I'd quit. The poor guy, I knew what a good gig I had, so I was never quitting. I was there for the next 15 years until that day.

Now that I was unemployed, I was able to focus on my stand-up comedy. It was the best of both worlds for me. Traveling can be terrible or terribly funny. I had such fun touring the country in theaters with my friends Karen Morgan and Sherry Davey with our comedy trio *Mama's Night Out*. I will always remember performing at the Majestic Theater in Gettysburg, Pennsylvania and staying at the Best Western. It was lovely. We had a sold-out show, big laughs, and a standing ovation. Afterwards, we went to the hotel bar for an after-show cocktail(s), and when we walked in, the entire room applauded. Everyone was buying us drinks. It was one of those rare, magical comedy nights when you feel like a rock star. I was the last one to leave the bar and crawl into bed.

At 9:30 the next morning there was pounding on my

door. It was Karen and Sherry: "You have to come downstairs now!" I staggered into the elevator, a little hung-over, and when the doors opened... I honestly thought I had died and woken up in another century. There were men in Confederate uniforms saluting each other, women in hoop skirts and bonnets, and a small boy with a fife and drum marching down the hall. I turned to Karen and Sherry and said, "How much did I drink last night? *What year is this?!*" We'd stumbled into a full-blown Civil War reenactment. I just kept thinking, that poor little boy probably said to his mother, "Mom, can't I just play soccer like my friends?" And she said, "No, son... you have to play your father into battle." The glamorous life of show business. One night you're a star, the next morning you're in 1863.

Little drummer boy and his parents before the battle

I also finally had time to do what I've always wanted to do, which was to go back to school, as long as I didn't have to take math. I attended NYU in New York City and got my Professional Certification in Life Coaching. I went on to write a book called *Who's Better Than Me?* I

Prescription: Laughter

then started giving humorous, inspirational speeches to my target audiences which, no surprise, ended up being nurses, teachers, volunteers and the "Do-Gooders" in the world. So though I never became a nurse, I was now able to inspire them, and give them a well-deserved laugh. One time after one of my speeches a Nursing Administrator came up to me and said, "Thank you for doing such a good deed in a nasty world." I always love that expression, and I say it often. Though I realized I'd never be Sister Antonio Maria, a nurse, St. Bernadette or Doris Day, I learned I could be a Do-Gooder for the Do-Gooders. I'll take it!

I think the hardest part of being a Do-Gooder is the fact that it requires you to deal with people. I remember being on a plane from New Orleans to New York and there was a young lady sitting next to me. We started up a conversation and she told me she had just graduated from Tulane University with a degree in English Literature. I asked her what she planned to do with her English degree, and she said, "I don't really know. I just know I love people, so I'd really love a job working with people." I looked at her a little amused and replied, "Well, obviously, you have never worked with people before. Because you'll be working with *people* for about two weeks and you'll be dying to get a job working with farm animals." We both had a good laugh and I don't think she understood that I was serious.

Because people can be exhausting and draining, I impress upon my audiences that they must take care of themselves. I ask them to imagine a well full of water, and every day people come for a dipper... your husband, boss, and kids, (though they'll come for a gallon not a dipper). Now if you keep giving without replenishing, the well will run bone-dry. That will make you feel terrible and it will make those that depend on you feel disappointed, too.

It's the same concept as when you are on an airplane, and they say, "In the event of a sudden loss of cabin pressure, oxygen masks will drop from the compartment above your seat. Pull the mask toward you to start the flow of oxygen. Place the mask over your nose and mouth, secure it with the elastic band, and breathe normally. Although the bag may not inflate, oxygen is flowing. Be sure to secure your own mask, before assisting others." You have to take care of yourself first before you can help others. My favorite line in there is: **Place the mask over your nose and mouth, secure it with the elastic band, and breathe normally**. All I know is if that oxygen mask pops in front of my face, I will do anything except... breathe normally.

We must be our own best friend. You don't have to wait around for your kids or your husbands to give you anything, you know better than anyone what will make you happy. I learned that one year when my kids chipped in and gave me a DNR bracelet to wear to the gym. I guess they never heard of Pandora! It's so important that we make time for ourselves. We don't need anyone to give it to us. "Would you *please* go up and take a bubble bath, have a nice drink, then take a long nap? You deserve it," said no one ever! Finding happi-

Prescription: Laughter

ness is your personal mission. Your family will thank you, your co-workers will thank you, and you'll be the biggest beneficiary of all.

Now please take a bath, or a nap and take your prescription for laughter, not from CVS, but from the jokes below.

Nancy Witter

PRESCRIPTION: Laughter

Peter worked in a pickle factory as a pickle slicer. He had been employed there for several years. One day he came home and confessed to his wife, Penelope, that he had an irresistible urge to stick his pecker into the pickle slicer. Penelope suggested to Peter that he should see a therapist to talk about it, but he vowed to overcome the compulsion on his own. A few weeks later, Peter came home and said, "Well, I did it!" "You did what?" Penelope asked. "Do you remember that I told you how I had this tremendous urge to put my pecker into the pickle slicer?" "Oh, Peter, you didn't!" she exclaimed. "Yes, I did," he replied. "My God! Peter, what happened?" He said, "I got fired." Then she urgently asked, "No, Peter, I mean, what happened with the pickle slicer?" He said, "Oh yeah ...she got fired too!"

A nurse walks into a bank. She goes into her purse to take out a pen but instead pulls out a rectal thermometer. She looks up at the teller, pauses for a moment, then realizing her mistake, she says, "Great… Some asshole's got my pen."

Prescription: Laughter

———

A elderly man is lying in bed in the hospital with an oxygen mask over his mouth. A young nurse appears to sponge his hands and feet. "Nurse," he mumbles from behind the mask, "Are my testicles black?" The young nurse replies, "I don't think so Mr. Smedley, you had an ankle repair." He struggles again to ask, "Nurse, are my testicles black?" Finally, she pulls back the covers, raises his gown, checks out the appropriate apparatus, and then puts everything back where she found it. She said "Mr. Smedley, as I suspected your testicles are not black, they are fine." Finally, the man pulls off his oxygen mask and says, "That was very nice but I said are... my... test... results... back?"

———

A nurse dies and goes to hell. The poor thing was there for two weeks before she realized she wasn't at work.

———

My father always used to say, "In life, one door might close, but another one will open." He was a great philosopher, but an awful cabinet builder.

———

A woman in her fifties is at home, happily humming and smiling as she is cooking. Her husband watches her for a while and asks, "What are you so happy about?" The woman continues to hum and smile and says, "I just came from having a mammogram, and the doctor says that I am healthy, and I have the breasts of an 18-year-old." The husband replies, "What did he say about your 55-year-old ass?" "Nothing …your name never came up."

Chapter 8

Oh Baby!

I've often heard that our parents are the blueprint we follow, when we begin to build and raise our own children. We think we will be so much better and that we won't make the same mistakes they did. But the truth is, history is a powerful teacher. It shapes us in ways we sometimes don't even realize until we hear our mother's words coming out of our own mouths. "If you don't turn down that music **RIGHT NOW**, I will hit you so hard, your kids will be born dizzy," and I thought ... *Did that come out of MY mouth?*

Each generation of new parents is very different. I was over the moon when my son, Michael, told me he and his wife, Patricia, were expecting my first grandchild. They were expecting a little girl named Ellie. My joy was short-lived, though, when he added, "We're planning a home water birth." I said, "Ahh, no you're not. You're not going to drown my first grandchild, and I can't save her because I'm not a lifeguard!"

Then I realized… this is just generational. Just as my mother would've been horrified by Lamaze, I was equally horrified by a home water birth. But it's a new generation and they're gonna do what they're gonna do. So I shut up, smiled, and got on board. Thank God, everything went flawlessly.

Mike & Baby Ellie

It did make me wonder, though, how did I ever buy into that Lamaze scam? I mean, who came up with that? I picture a big medical conference back in the day. The moderator says, "Okay doctors, last item before lunch. Any new ideas for pain management during childbirth?"

A hand goes up in the back. "Yes, Dr. Lamaze?" He says, "How about… breathing?" The moderator: "Brilliant! That's lunch, everyone!" The fact that women bought into that just shows how amazing we women are.

Prescription: Laughter

We'll endure and sacrifice anything if we think it's in the best interest of our babies.

Now men? They'd never go for this. Picture it: a guy walks into the doctor's office, the nurse says, "Right this way, Mr. Jones." The doctor smiles and says, "Hello Mr. Jones, have a seat. Today we're going to be doing your vasectomy, but we are going to be doing something a little different. Today we will not be using any anesthesia, but don't worry about a thing, because we are going to teach you how to breathe through the pain." That man would be out of there faster than a drag queen at a Republican convention.

Today is so different from my mother or from me. Parents-to-be know the sex of the baby at two months, exactly when it's going to be born, and many babies have made their Instagram debut (sonogram) before they were even born. They have a name picked out and many are enrolled in kindergarten before the first trimester.

Everything is so confusing these days. If you want to really get confused go to brunch with my daughter Annie and her friends in Brooklyn. They call themselves millennials … I call them idiots. Oh.. the poor waiter. The first one starts to order and says "I'm going to need something Keto friendly." I didn't know food had personality traits. The next one said, "I need something gluten free." Then another, "I'm a vegetarian." Now I see it is getting ratcheted up. The next one says "I'm a vegan" and the next "I'm a pescatarian." I said. "I'm a Catholic, what difference does it make?"

Then when we left I said to Annie, "That Amy and

Jonathan make such a cute couple." She rolled her eyes and said, "They're not a couple, Mom." I said "I thought they were a couple." Annie said "They're not because Amy is polyamorous." Now it was my turn to roll my eyes and I said "What exactly does that mean?" She said indignantly "It means… she can love several people at the same time." I said "In my day… we called that a slut." Annie shouted, "That's poly shaming, Mom." I said "Yes it is… Yes… it is." Sometimes there aren't enough hormones to get me through brunch.

Names have also changed over the years. The most common names when I was growing up were Carol, Barbara, Cathy, Lisa, and of course the iconic Karen. Today you can name your child literally anything you want. I think Gwyneth Paltrow started this. She named her daughter Apple. I don't know whether that was because she liked computers, or fruit. Then the Beckhams came along and named their son Brooklyn. Please don't get me started on Elon Musk. He named his child after a math equation!

A few weeks ago, I visited my daughter's best friend who just had a baby girl. She introduced me to the baby and told me her name is Hydrangea, but that they're going to call her Heidi. Now in my head, I thought, *Why don't you skip Hydrangea and go straight to Heidi so you don't sound ya know…insane!* But instead I said, "That is so original. What inspired you to name her Hydrangea?" She said, "I just love hydrangeas and I love my daughter." I really believe she thought that made the greatest amount of sense. I thought to myself, *If my mother had named me after the things she loved in 1956, my name would have been Parliament, and my brother would have been named Schlitz!*

The infant seat, which was a miracle of a product when it became mandatory in 1979, was non-existent when I was growing up. I remember going to church with my mother and my father and seven kids in a Dodge Dart with no seatbelts. We sat four in the front, four in the back and baby Peanut in the back window. My mother also smoked in the car and if it was raining, the windows were up. I bet I had stage four COPD by the time I was five! We all went to Catholic school, so Mass on Sunday was mandatory. I hated it whenever I ran into my nun, Sister Betrille, because it was so hard to curtsey and flinch at the same time.

Schools are so different now. When Ellie had her birthday I said to my son, "Do you want me to make cupcakes for Ellie to bring to school?" He said, "Absolutely not, cupcakes aren't even allowed in the school. You don't know what allergies the kids might have and they are just full of sugar and gluten." I said, "Well that's the best part of the cupcake!" I think if I walked into a school with a jar of peanut butter, I would be arrested as a domestic terrorist.

My grandchildren are way more advanced in technology than I am, even at 3-years-old. I mean, it really boggles the mind. They don't know how to tie their shoes, but I'll tell you this… my little Ellie built me the most beautiful website.

No matter the gadgets, monitors, or miracle bassinets, babies still wake up crying at 2:00 a.m. Parents have been pacing the floor in their pajamas for centuries. Some things never change. Thank God! They say the days are long but the years are short. Blink and they are all grown up. Enjoy the journey!

My Irish twins today

If you are pacing the floor with a baby, or just resting from busy days, here is your prescription for laughter. Enjoy the jokes!

PRESCRIPTION: Laughter

"Having children is like living in a frat house. Nobody sleeps, everything is broken, and there's a lot of throwing up." *Ray Romano*

———

Having a daughter is like having a broke friend who thinks you're rich.

———

My daughter is not the sharpest knife in the drawer. She went to the bank to open a checking account and the banker was filling out the forms and asked her what her birth date was and she said "December 22nd." The banker said, "What year?" She replied, "It's every year isn't it?"

———

Little Johnny was in Bible study one morning. Sally was sleeping in front of Johnny. The teacher asked Sally who our Lord and Savior was. Little Johnny poked her in the butt with a pin and she screamed, "Jesus Christ!" And fell back to sleep. A little while later the teacher asked Sally who created our world. Johnny poked her in the butt again and Sally screamed, "Oh, my God!" And fell back to sleep. Later the teacher asked Sally what Eve said to Adam after they had their 3rd son. Johnny poked her in the butt once again and Sally screamed, "If you stick that thing in me one more time I'm gonna break it!" The teacher fainted.

A young teacher is supervising the children in the lunchroom when she sees Jimmy making ugly faces at another child. She looks at Jimmy sternly and says "Jimmy, when I was a young girl I was told that if I made ugly faces for too long my face would stay that way." He looked up at the teacher and said "Well, you can't say that you weren't warned."

Jimmy is a 16-year-old and so is his girlfriend, Maggie. Maggie says, "We've been going out for so long that tonight I want you to come to my house for dinner and meet my parents. Then, when they go to bed, we'll go downstairs and tell them we're watching TV but we will make love for the first time." Then she says, "but Jimmy, you must take care of protection." He was very excited and went off to the pharmacy. He talked to the pharmacist and explained his situation. The pharmacist said there are several types of protection you can choose

Prescription: Laughter

from, and they come in a four pack, six pack, or ten pack. He said, "Since this is our first time, I think I'll take the ten pack." Then he promptly went over to his girlfriend's house. He was late and the family was already sitting at the dining room table when he arrived. The mother said to Jimmy, "Since you're our guest tonight, you can say grace." Jimmy starts to say grace and goes on for well over ten minutes. When he was done his girlfriend leaned over and whispered, "I had no idea you were so religious." Jimmy looks at her, gulps and says, "I had no idea your father was a pharmacist."

―――

Yesterday, my mother asked me to hand out the invitations for my brother's surprise birthday party. That's when I realized that he was her favorite twin.

Chapter 9
Bombs Away!

Once in a while when I would get together with my comedy friends, we'd reminisce about some of our most memorable shows. We never talked about the good ones, there was no fun in that. We loved to discuss the disasters and we would almost try to outdo each other to see who had the worst experience. Little did I know that all we were doing was reframing something that wasn't funny, into something hilarious. I think sometimes, how much fun that would be if we could try that in corporate America. People could sit around at a meeting and talk about the worst presentation they ever did or the worst sales pitch they ever delivered. I think it's a missed opportunity, because when you lose, don't lose the lesson. There's a lot to be learned by your mistakes, because those are the lessons you remember the most.

I remember going to one of my first comedy gigs. I was on the subway with my sister Ditta going to Stand-

Prescription: Laughter

Up NY. It was maybe my third show and she turned to me and said, "Aren't you afraid you might bomb?" And I said, "No…but thanks for bringing it up." Then I went on to explain to her my philosophy. I said, "I think I feel the same as a surgeon must feel when performing open heart surgery. He wouldn't go into surgery if he didn't believe the patient would survive. However, as we all know, once in a while the patient doesn't survive, no matter how prepared, confident or optimistic the surgeon may have been. Just like the surgeon (I love comparing myself to a surgeon), every time I get on stage, I assume I'm going to do great. It doesn't mean I always do, but I have to believe I will or I'd never get the nerve to go on stage.

Here is one of my favorite comedy disaster stories. There was a friend of mine, Michael, who was very involved in nonprofit charities in New York City. We did comedy together for years. I was in my 40s and he was in his 50s. He did comedy more as a hobby. He called me one day and said, "I have a gig for you. It's a St. Patrick's Day charity event and people will donate money and you will tell a joke in their honor and we'll raise a lot of money." At the time most of my act was about growing up in a very large Irish Catholic family, so I agreed to do it.

The day of the event I went to Tribeca to a very high-end art gallery. Everyone was standing around drinking fancy champagne with a big strawberry in it, and it looked like it was going to be a very easy gig.

The chairman of the event got up, then he got

everyone's attention by clinking his champagne glass. When everyone was quiet, he started, "I want to thank you all for coming. We've raised a lot of money for a very good cause and I'm very excited to have Michael and Nancy here to entertain us. But before we start with the jocularity…I have an announcement to make." As soon as I heard this, I got a queasy feeling in my stomach. I noticed him blinking a lot and his voice sounded like it might crack so I knew nothing good was coming. Then he started again, "I don't know how many of you knew Susan Clark, but she was our boots on the ground, giving humanitarian aid in Nicaragua. Last week she was killed by a bunch of insurgents, leaving behind her husband and a three month old baby." And then he broke down. Everyone around the room looked at each other in shock and all I could hear was, "Oh no, not Susan!" The next thing I know a box of tissues appeared and was being passed around the room. The chairman finally composed himself enough to say, "And now I would like to introduce to you the host of the evening, our friend Michael." I looked Michael in the eye, as if to say, *Do your job and try to get the room back.* Obviously he couldn't read my eyes because Michael got up and said, "I knew Susan very well and I can honestly say her loss will leave a void in the world that I don't think will ever be filled. So, in honor of Susan, I think we should have a moment of silence." That gave me a little time to think. I thought I'd have more time to think after the moment of silence.

When it was finished, Michael was supposed to perform comedy for 5 or 10 minutes to warm up the crowd. I thought by then the room would have composed itself and then I could tell my plethora of Irish jokes that I was paid for. Instead, when the moment of silence was finished, Michael looked up at the crowd and said, "And now I know you will all enjoy the comedy stylings of Nancy Witter!" I looked around the room and people were still comforting each other, many still had their arms around each other, there was a lot of sniffling and nose blowing. I was panicking trying to figure out how I was going to gracefully go from tragedy to comedy with no time in-between. So I got up, I looked around the room and I just grabbed for any words I could and I said, "I didn't know Susan, but she sounds like a brave and generous soul. When I heard this story, I realized, in life, that is the rain… and tonight…I am the rainbow." Then with no hesitation I just started with, "An Irishman walks out of a bar… It could happen! That joke was donated by Eddie O'Connor. Thank you Eddie!" and I just went on from there. By the end I could tell I killed, not because they were laughing, but because they were no longer crying. That was 25 years ago and I never forgot a minute of it. It is also where you get your comedy muscle from, because later on in my career something similar happened two or three other times. Each time, I was able to successfully pull out of my pocket the old "rain to rainbow" bit.

There are so many shows where things go sideways and you have to think on your feet. I was doing a show at Country Club and it was a women's night out event. They had little snacks for the ladies on the table and drinks were being delivered. It was a fun and lively event. I got up and whatever I said must have been very funny because a poor woman had a pretzel nugget in her mouth and when she laughed, she inhaled it and it got stuck in her windpipe. So in the middle of the act, I heard a commotion and suddenly someone got up, went over and delivered the Heimlich maneuver. EMS was called to make sure she was ok and happily she walked out of the room with her friends. I had to continue after the near-death experience. I met with her after the show. She was lying on a couch in a private room at the club and all she was upset about was if she'd ruined the show. I said, "Absolutely not. I'm just so happy you are fine, and so sorry I almost killed you. If I did, it would have given me a great credential. I could have honestly said, 'I did a gig and I literally killed,' but I'm so glad I didn't."

Finding the funny in failure or even an unexpected or awkward moment on stage, has an upside. When you laugh at a bad situation, you take away its sting. Reframing a flop, a mistake, or awkward moment as comedy reduces its emotional weight. Suddenly, instead of being crushed by embarrassment or frustration, you're in control and you've turned the problem into the punchline.

Comedians who bomb and laugh about it instead of crumbling, often come back stronger. The same is true in life. If you can joke about your own disaster, you've proven to yourself you can survive it and even own it. Actually, people love when someone can laugh at themselves. Sharing a story of a "so-bad-it's-funny" moment

Prescription: Laughter

makes you more human and approachable. Instead of isolating you, the experience bonds you with others because everyone has their own version of a flop, and humor invites them to laugh *with* you, not *at* you.

I am prescribing you a dose of laughter, and I hope I don't bomb!

Nancy Witter

PRESCRIPTION: Laughter

A magician is on stage and asks an audience member to help him with his final trick. Bob is chosen and goes on stage. The magician hands Bob a baseball bat and instructs him to hit him as hard as he can against his head. Bob says he can't do that and that he is too uncomfortable and afraid he will hurt the magician. The magician assured him he is a professional and knows exactly what he is doing and once again implores Bob to hit him with the baseball bat as hard as he can. Bob does it and the magician's head splits open with blood pouring out, he is knocked unconscious and falls into a coma. Bob is by his side day and night for two weeks, when suddenly the magician slowly awakens. He turns and the first person he sees is Bob. He looks at Bob and spreads his arms and says, "Ta…. Daaaa!"

———

A married couple is at the zoo. They come across the gorilla enclosure. The gorilla looks at the wife and starts pounding on his chest. The husband says to the wife, "I think he has the hots for you. Show him a little leg." The wife does that and the gorilla goes nuts. Then the husband says, "Show him a little shoulder," and so she does a little shimmy and the gorilla goes insane. Then the husband opens the enclosure and pushes his wife in, and says to her, "Now… tell him you have a headache!"

———

Bob was in trouble. He forgot his wedding anniversary. His wife was really angry. She told him, "Tomorrow morning, I expect to find a gift in the driveway that goes from 0 to 200 in 6 seconds AND IT BETTER BE THERE!" The next morning he got up early and left for work. When his wife woke up, she looked out the window and sure enough there was a box gift-wrapped in the middle of the driveway. Confused, the wife put on her robe and ran out to the driveway, and brought the box back into the house. She opened it and found a brand new bathroom scale. Bob is still in the hospital, but is expected to make a full recovery.

———

A man walks into a bar with his dog and orders three beers. When he is done, the bartender says, "That'll be $6.00." The man says, "I'm sorry I don't have any money but I have a talking dog, and it's worth seeing for $6.00." The bartender agrees to see the dog. So the man says "What sits on top of a house?" And the dog barks, "Roof roof." The bartender says, "That's terrible." Then the man says to the dog, "How does sandpaper feel?" and the dog says, "Ruff ruff." The bartender says, "I'll give you one more chance before I throw you out of here." So the man asks the dog, "Who is the greatest baseball player of all time?" and the dog says "Ruth Ruth." The bartender then throws them both out of the bar. The dog then looks up at his owner and says, "Do you think I should have said Shohei Ohtani?"

―――

A senior citizen in Florida bought a brand new Corvette convertible. He took off down the road, flooring it to 80 mph. Then he looked in his rear view mirror and saw a highway patrol trooper behind him, blue lights flashing and siren blaring. He thought, *I can get away from him with no problem*, and he floored it some more and flew down the road at over 100 mph. Then 110, 120 mph. Then he thought, *What am I doing? I'm too old for this kind of thing.* He pulled over to the side of the road and waited for the trooper to catch up with him. The trooper pulled in behind the Corvette and walked up to the man. "Sir," he said, looking at his watch. "My shift ends in 30 minutes and today is Friday. If you can give me a good reason why you were speeding that I've never heard before, I'll let you go." The man looked at the trooper and said, "Years ago my wife ran off with a Florida State Trooper, and I thought you were bringing her back." "Have a good day, Sir," said the Trooper.

―――

A man and his wife are driving down the highway. They get pulled over by the police. The policeman goes to the

Prescription: Laughter

side of the car and says to the husband who was driving, "Sir, I pulled you over because you were going 75 mph in a 55 mile an hour zone." The husband said, "I'm sorry officer. This is a brand new car and I had no idea how powerful it was." The wife then leaned over and said, "That's a lie officer. We've had this car for three years. He always speeds." The husband turned to his wife and screamed, "Shut your ugly face, I'm talking here." The police officer was very surprised. Then he said to the husband, "Sir, I also noticed you didn't have your seatbelt on." The husband quickly replied, "Oh no, officer. I had it on the whole time. I just took it off when I saw you coming to the side of the car so I could take out my identification for you." The wife then chimed in again and said, "That's another lie officer. I yell at him all the time because he never wears his seatbelt." Then the husband turned to her again and said, "You stupid old, ugly woman, I told you before to keep your pie-hole shut!" The officer then leaned over toward the woman and said, "Does your husband always talk to you like that?" She smiled slyly and said, "No officer… only when he's been drinking."

Chapter 10
There's A Bear In My Bed!

My sisters were my first friends and are still my best friends. They knew me before I even knew myself. They saw me under construction and there's a comfort in having people who knew me, before I became me. Nothing can compare to the bond of sisters.

Sisters will always tell you the truth. They will tell you if you have a piece of tissue clinging to your heel or if you have spinach in your teeth. They'll tell you that you look good in flats and you don't need to wear Spanx to their daughter's wedding.

Carol is the oldest sister and she has always shown up for all of us. After my mother died, Carol was the one that showed up at my annual Christmas concert. With so many kids, especially me being number six of seven, my parents were not enthusiastic about attending school events. It never really bothered me until after my mother died. I became more aware of the entourage of

Prescription: Laughter

family that showed up for my classmates to cheer them on and I was a little envious. Carol must have sensed this, because at the concert I looked down and there she was sitting in the front row. I was so happy and proud that I had an entourage, too. Carol took me out for the requisite ice cream at Howard Johnson's after the show. This is something Carol might never remember, and yet it is something that I'll never forget.

When I was nominated for a New York City, MAC (Manhattan Association of Cabarets) Award for Outstanding Female Comedian, my sister Carol flew in from Bismarck, North Dakota to be at the award show. She was tasked with getting me dressed for the show. Normally that wouldn't be too hard, but my back was out and I couldn't even bend down to put my shoes on. So she helped me from pulling up my panty hose to putting on my heels. The poor thing! She was an even better sport because after I won, I dragged her to parties all around the city. The first place we went I introduced her to some Drag Queens. She thought they were stun...ning! I had to remind her they were also men. Then we saw Peggy Lee and Judy Garland perform. Peggy Lee sang *Is That All There Is* and Judy sang *Somewhere Over The Rainbow*. Carol leaned over to me and said "I thought they were dead," and I said, "Only in real life, Carol." She was just as comfortable at a gay club as she was in the frozen food aisle of her grocery store on a Tuesday afternoon. She sure did have some great stories to tell when she got back to Bismarck.

Over the years, my older sister Ditta, has been my

biggest cheerleader and my greatest supporter. It's like that old Mastercard commercial, "Taking your sister to a comedy show… $25, buying her drinks…$50, having someone in the audience to laugh when no one else does… priceless!"

This is one of the most classic Ditta stories. In the early 2000s Ditta was dating a man named Larry. He owned quite a few buildings in town and when they would pass one, he'd point and say "I own that building." The next time they spotted another one of his buildings, he would once again say "I own that building." One day they were driving to my cousin Lizzie's house in Fairfield, Connecticut for a family party. They came up on the Hutchinson River Parkway in Westchester County and on the side of the road was a sign that said "Iona College." Larry noticed the sign and said to Ditta as he pointed "Oh look, Iona College." Ditta, not even looking, turned to him and said incredulously "You own a college???"

My sister Peanut was my first roommate as we shared a room together growing up. Whenever we get together with family, my job is to tell "Peanut stories." She is so kind and generous with her time, love and energy and is the greatest hostess I've ever known. She makes everyone feel at home, and welcomed.

Prescription: Laughter

Peanut is the type of person who knows everything about the waiter by the time we pay the bill. She's sweet, talkative and truly interested whether they are checking her out at Trader Joe's or Home Goods. She is another one that shows up. When I had a big 60th birthday show at a local event space, Peanut not only came from Cary, North Carolina to see it, she brought her daughters, their mothers-in-law and all of her local friends from high school. Yep, she is still friends with them 40 years later. Whenever I have an important show, she gathers her gaggle of friends and packs the place.

Peanut was the baby in the family and I think my brothers and sisters would agree that Peanut was my mother's favorite and, quite frankly, everybody's favorite, even to this day. She was called Peanut from the day she was born because she was so little, and still is. Most people don't know her real name is Maryann. Peanut and I were only 16 months apart. So every Easter my mother dressed us like matching Fabergé eggs. She took Easter fashion as seriously as Anna Wintour takes the Met Gala, except with a tighter budget and more pastels.

Peanut and I would walk together to the school bus stop every day. One day it was very windy and my mother stood at the door as we left, waving goodbye but looking very worried. Then we heard her voice cut through the wind and she said "Peannny… be careful I don't want you to blow away." And there was a pause and the next thing she said was "Hold on to Nancy!" So Peanut was the damsel in distress and I saved the day because suddenly I was a human anchor.

We always loved being together and being with our cousins. One of my favorite adventures involved a motel room somewhere off the New Jersey turnpike in 2003. It was late January and my cousin Dee Dee had a party at her beautiful home in Freehold, New Jersey. My sister Ditta had just purchased a Subaru from Craigslist. She really is the most resourceful person I know. I believe it had 150,000 miles on it and I thought she was crazy to buy a car with so many miles, but then she assured me that a Subaru with 150,000 miles on it is the same as a Ford with 70,000 miles on it and they last forever. I asked her where she saw that, but she just ignored me.

We decided that night to stay at a Red Roof Inn down the road as it got late early. It was the kind of place where you parked your car in front of your door. So my sisters and I walked into this freezing cold room. There were tiles on the floor and very suspect looking bedspreads. Thank God we didn't have a black light because who knows what was on those things! We started laughing about how horrible the room was when all of a sudden we heard this God awful **Yeehaw Yeehaw Yeehaw.** It was Ditta's Subaru's car alarm going off. We said, "Ditta go turn the alarm off." She said, "I don't know how. I didn't even know there was an alarm." We said, "Go get the manual and we'll see if we can figure it out." Ditta looked at us and replied, "There is no manual!" We were laughing so hard at 2 o'clock in the morning we thought we were going to get thrown out of the Red Roof Inn, which would have been a special kind of humiliation. Then, all of a sudden, the honking stopped. We were so relieved and just as we were getting into bed, it started again. We went out and opened up the hood for no good reason, because we know nothing about cars, then just slammed it down and miraculously it stopped.

I got into bed with Peanut and Ditta got into bed

with Carol. We turned off the lights and the room was now pitch black. Then Ditta got up to go to the bathroom. Because the room was so cold, Ditta decided on the way back to bed to put on her mink coat that Larry had just given to her for Christmas. In the dark Ditta slipped back into bed, and then all of a sudden, Carol let out a blood curdling scream **"THERE'S A BEAR IN MY BED…THERE'S A BEAR IN MY BED!"** We all panicked. I reached over as fast as I could to turn on the lights as we all scrambled out of bed ready to run out the door. Then we looked up and there was Ditta standing in her full-length mink coat, twisting her head left and right and shouting **"WHERE'S THE BEAR??? WHERE'S THE BEAR???"** Carol just stared at her and asked her incredulously, "What, in the name of God, are you doing in your mink coat in bed?" Ditta said "When I got up to go to the bathroom, it was freezing, so I thought it was a good idea to put my coat on to keep me warm." The next thing we hear is **Yeehaw Yeehaw Yeehaw**, and then again for no good reason after five minutes, apropos of nothing, it just stopped. We all fell back on our beds and almost died laughing.

That was 20 years ago. It's these kinds of memories that keep the four of us so close and remind us, as my mother always said, "that we're very lucky to have each other."

Prescription: Laughter

Left to right Carol, Ditta, Nancy, Peanut

Now here's your prescription, read these jokes and enjoy the belly laugh.

Nancy Witter

PRESCRIPTION: Laughter

Bob walked into a sports bar around 5:58 p.m.. He sat down next to a very attractive blonde at the bar and stared up at the TV. The 6:00 p.m. news was coming on. The news crew was covering the story of a man on the ledge of a large building preparing to jump. Bob said, "I'll bet you $20 he jumps." The blonde replied, "Well, I'll bet $20 he won't jump." The blonde kept watching the scene on TV. The guy on the ledge did a swan dive off the building, falling to his death. The blonde was very upset, but willingly handed her $20 to Bob. "Fair's fair. Here's your money." Bob replied, "I can't take your money, I saw this earlier on the 5:00 p.m. news, so I knew he would jump." The blonde replied, "I did, too, but I didn't think he'd do it again."

―――――

An Amish man is visiting a mall with his wife and young son for the first time. The wife leaves them to go into Victoria's Secret. The father and son find themselves in front of an elevator, they don't know what it is. Suddenly the door opens and an elderly woman gets in. The door then closes, and the two don't know what to make of it. A few minutes go by and suddenly the same door opens again and out walks a beautiful 20-year-old woman. The father looks at his son and says, "Quick, get your mother."

A beautiful blonde boards an airliner and sits down in First Class. The flight attendant checks her ticket and says, "This ticket is for economy, you'll have to move." The blonde says, "I'm blonde, I'm beautiful, and I'm going to New York in First Class." The flight attendant once again reminds her that she has a seat in economy and did not pay for a First Class ticket. They continued to argue back and forth for a few minutes. She kept repeating "I'm blonde, I'm beautiful, and I'm going to New York in First Class." Finally, the flight attendant goes to the pilot and tells him the trouble she is having. The pilot says, "Did you say she was blonde?" "Yes," the flight attendant replied. "I'll take care of it, my wife is blonde. I speak blonde." He goes over to the blonde, whispers something in her ear, and immediately she says, "Oh, thank you so much Captain." Then the blonde gets up and goes to her proper seat in economy. The flight attendant said "That was remarkable Captain, what did you say to her?" He said "I told her that First Class was going to Germany, and Economy was going to New York!"

Mary is on a BBC reality dating show. The host asks Mary, "Now Mary, if you were stranded on a deserted island, who would you like to be deserted with?" "My uncle Mike," replies Mary. The host is puzzled and asks, "Now why of all the men you choose would you choose your Uncle Mike?" She looks at him and says, "Because he's got a frigging boat."

———

A blonde pushes her BMW into a gas station. She tells the mechanic it died. After he works on it for a few minutes, it is idling smoothly. She says, "What's the story?" He replies, "Just crap in the carburetor." She asks, "How often do I have to do that?"

———

Two cannibals are eating a clown. One says to the other, "Does this taste funny to you?"

———

A couple are rushing into the hospital because the wife is going into labor. As they walk in, a doctor says to them that he has invented a machine that splits the pain between the mother and father. They agree to it and are led into a room where they get hooked up to the machine. The doctor starts it off at 20% split towards the father. The wife says, "Oh, that's actually better." The husband says he can't feel anything. Then the doctor turns it to 50% and the wife says that it doesn't hurt nearly as much. The husband says he still can't feel anything. The Doctor, now encouraged, turns it up to 100%. The husband still can't feel anything, and the wife is really happy, because there is now no pain for her. The baby is born. The couple go home and find the postman groaning in pain on the doorstep.

———

A man calls 911 and says, "Please send an ambulance right away. My wife is in labor." The 911 operator asks, "Is this her first child?" He says, "No you idiot… this is her husband."

———

An English teacher has volunteered to educate prisoners at a local prison. The teacher asked, "Can you tell me please, what comes after every sentence?" One of the prisoners then responded "That's easy. Parole."

Chapter 11
Rain, Rome And Raphael

When you reach a certain age, you realize you better travel while you still can. Traveling teaches you so much, especially if you know very little.

I went to Rome with my two best friends, Carol and Cathy. One of the first places we went to was the Trevi Fountain. After several glasses of wine, I referred to it as the Trivia Fountain…that Italian wine is delicious! The next place we went was the Pantheon. While we were there, the tour guide kept referring to Raphael. I turned to my two well-educated friends and said "Who is Raphael? Why do they keep talking about him?" My friend Cathy rolled her eyes and said "You don't know who Raphael is?" I said "The only Raphael I know is a Teenage Mutant Ninja Turtle." Cathy then asked me "And who were his friends?" I replied "Leonardo, Michelangelo, Donatello and ohhhh….Raphael was an artist?!?" Cathy looked at me and said "That's how you know that?" I said "Everything I ever learned, I learned from TV."

We went to the Vatican and there was a lot of learning to do there. Then the next day we went to the Colosseum, and we splurged and got a private tour guide. I peppered this poor guy with every question I could think of. He also took us to the Mausoleum of Augustus where Marcus Agrippa was buried. The guide told us "He had been married to Julia, Augustus's daughter, after the death of her first husband, Marcellus. Agrippa's death occurred in 12 BC." I waved my hand in the air to ask another question. He was a little exasperated by then and said "Yes... Nancy?" I said "When did they start counting time? I mean just like 12 years before they decided to start counting time?" He shook his head, took a deep breath and tried to gather all the patience he could muster and said, "That is a very big subject Nancy and there are many books in the library that will explain the complicated history of global calendars." I said "Yeah that's okay I wasn't *that* interested, it's just that history is like a murder mystery because I don't know the ending of anything. It's all new to me."

Nancy Witter

Cathy, Carol (in the middle), Nancy… off to Rome!

I love traveling with my sisters, too. One day, my cousin Dee Dee called and proposed that my sisters and I join her on a trip to Paris. We thought it was a great idea so off we went. Ditta couldn't make it, and we missed her. Dee Dee is like our 5th sister. Actually Dee Dee, Carol, Ditta, and Peanut all went to the University of Dayton in Ohio where Carol and Peanut were crowned Homecoming Queens. I am the only one of my sisters who didn't go to the University of Dayton, and the only one who married someone from the University of Dayton. Dee Dee is funny, kind and thoughtful. She has the greatest laugh and is generous in every way. No matter where we go, Dee starts a conversation with any stranger and manages to close the gap of the six degrees of separation. The classic story about Dee Dee is that she was at a wedding, and it was a very hot day. And she went up to the bar and said to the bartender, "Can I just get a cold glass of water?" and he said, "S. Pellegrino?" And she said, "No D. Andrejewski." (By the way S. Pellegrino is a sparkling water.)

We made the trip to Paris in May. We loved the city

of Paris and enjoyed the wine, croissants and all the favorite tourist destinations. We decided to leave the city for a day to go see the Palace of Versailles. We wanted to see the beautiful gardens and the iconic Hall of Mirrors. We got up, made our way to the train, and the minute we got off the train in Versailles the skies opened to a torrential rain storm. We had to walk about a half a mile to get to the Palace. By the time we got there, we were literally soaked to the bone and had to wait outside until it was our turn to enter. We walked around the Palace, leaving puddles everywhere we went. You could hear our shoes squishing, with every step we took. The Palace did not disappoint, it was beautiful! Sadly, we couldn't see the gardens because by now they were flooded. So we started walking back to the train and to get there we had to climb up a big hill . It was there that we saw a woman in a wheelchair, all by herself, who was struggling to go up that hill in the torrential rain. The four of us got behind that wheelchair and pushed her up and into the train station where at least she would be out of the rain. There we were with our hair matted and our clothes soaked to the skin. We looked at this poor woman and Dee Dee said "Are you alright?" And she just looked up and in her French accent said "And you thought you had it bad!" and we all laughed. That was the line of the day! It just goes to show, when you think you have it bad, there is always someone that has it much worse.

When we got on the train we looked at each other and saw there was a little river down by our feet, it was literally flowing down the aisle of the train. We couldn't look at each other without collapsing with laughter. We were so waterlogged, and it was so ridiculous that it was hilarious. We all would have preferred a beautiful day and a stroll through the lovely gardens. But because we were together, the rain didn't ruin our day, it made it! Another adventure we will remember… for as long as we can!

In Versailles left to right Peanut, Carol, Nancy, Dee Dee

I know as bad as things may be, with the right attitude, we can usually laugh our way out of it. If everything was perfect there would be no badge of honor for surviving it, and worst of all in a perfect world there would be nothing memorable and nothing to laugh at. The disasters and challenges we get through together are the memories that bind us. It's where love grows, and where the best memories live.

Now take a spoonful of sugar to make the medicine go down, your prescription of laughter is in the jokes below.

PRESCRIPTION: Laughter

Two sisters are sitting at the Oyster Bar in Grand Central Station having a martini at 2 o'clock in the afternoon. One of the sisters looked across the bar and saw two other elderly women having a martini and she turned to her sister and said, "See those two old broads? In 20 years that'll be us." Her sister looked at her and said, "You idiot, that's a mirror."

———

A man and his wife were having some problems at home and were giving each other the silent treatment. The next week, the man realized that he would need his wife to wake him at 5:00 a.m. for an early morning business flight to Chicago. Not wanting to be the first to break the silence (and lose), he wrote on a piece of paper, "Please wake me at 5:00 a.m.." The next morning the man woke up, only to discover it was 9:00 a.m. and that he had missed his flight. Furious, he was about to go and see why his wife hadn't awakened him, when he noticed a piece of paper by the bed. The paper said: "It is 5:00 a.m. Wake up."

———

My wife and I got into a conversation about life and death, and the need for living wills. During the course of the conversation I told her that I never wanted to exist in a vegetative state, dependent on some machine and taking fluids from a bottle. She got up and unplugged the TV.

―――

Sally was driving home in Arizona when she saw an elderly Navajo woman walking on the side of the road. She stopped and asked the Navajo woman if she would like a ride. Sally tried to make small talk with the Navajo woman, but the old woman just sat silently, looking intently at everything she saw, studying every little detail, until she noticed a brown bag on the seat next to Sally. "What in bag?" asked the old woman. Sally looked down at the brown bag and said, "It's a bottle of wine. I got it for my husband." The Navajo woman was silent for another moment or two. Then speaking with the quiet wisdom of an elder, she said: "Good trade…"

―――

When I went to lunch today, I noticed an old lady sitting on a park bench sobbing her eyes out. I stopped and asked her what was wrong. She said, "I have a 22-year-old husband at home. He makes love to me every morning and then gets up and makes me pancakes, sausage, fresh fruit and freshly ground coffee." I said, "Well, then why are you crying?" She said, "He makes me homemade soup for lunch and my favorite brownies and then makes love to me for half the afternoon. I said, "Well, why are you crying?" She said, "For dinner he makes me a gourmet meal with wine and my favorite dessert and then makes love to me until 2:00 am." I said, "Well, why in the world would you be crying? She said, "I can't remember where I live!"

A young boy says to his Dad, "Dad what is a man?" The father says "Son, a man is someone who is strong yet gentle and who supports and sacrifices for his family. A man is someone who listens and encourages his children, and most of all a man is someone who loves his family with his whole heart and would do anything to protect them." The young boy looked up at his Dad and said "Oh boy, when I grow up I wanna be a man…just like Mom."

A blonde, wanting to earn some extra money, decided to hire herself out as a "handy woman" and started canvassing a nearby well-to-do neighborhood. She went to the front door of the first house, and asked the owner if he had any odd jobs for her to do. "Well, I guess I could use somebody to paint my porch. How much will you charge me?" The blonde quickly responded, "How about $50?" The man agreed and told her that the paint and everything she would need was in the garage. The man's wife, hearing the conversation, said to her husband, "Does she realize that our porch goes all the way around the house?" He responded, "That's a bit cynical, isn't it?" The wife replied, "You're right. I guess I'm starting to believe all those 'dumb blonde' jokes we've been getting by e-mail lately." A short time later, the blonde came to the door to collect her money. "You're finished already?" the husband asked. "Yes," the blonde replied, "and I had paint left over, so I gave it two coats." Impressed, the man reached into his pocket for the $50 and handed it to her. "And by the way," the blonde added, "it's not a Porsche, it's a Lexus."

Chapter 12
Spanx For The Memories

It is more fun and beneficial to reframe any setback in a more positive way. I've had a lifelong battle with my weight and my biggest setbacks always came from my attempts at dieting. Many years ago I went to Jenny Craig. The salesperson said to me "Nancy, do you know the secret to losing weight?" and I looked at her and said "obviously not." She said, "you have to be honest with yourself." I didn't know lying to myself was so fattening! Then she said, "Here at Jenny Craig we will help you lose the weight but you have to have a realistic goal. I think our six-month program is ideal for you and will only cost you $550, not including food. It's an investment in yourself. So now, Nancy, what do you realistically expect to lose here at Jenny Craig? Remember now, be honest with yourself." I thought about it and I said "$550, not including food."

After Jenny Craig, I joined Weight Watchers and I have been on Weight Watchers for… 34 years and all I have ever lost is… hope. When I joined my last class, I was very lucky, because it happened to be a very fat class… I mean, I was their goal! I felt so skinny next to them and for that short amount of time, I knew what it felt like to be a super model. Compared to them I looked like I could have rickets, or needed someone to have a fundraiser for me. Thinking I was skinny brought out the worst in me. I'd walk past these people to get to the scale and I'd say, "excuse me, tubby." Then when I left the class and I was out among the general population I would think, *OMG, I totally forgot I have to lose 40 pounds!* I was reminded of that when people who walked past me would say, "Excuse me, tubby," to ME! A little bit of power, and a lot of delusion is a dangerous thing. The lesson is be careful who you compare yourself to. If I compare myself to Ariana Grande, I am morbidly obese, but if I compare myself to Lizzo, I'm just a slip of a girl. Run your own race and stay in your own lane.

I am very good at justifying anything, from eating too much, to missing a gym class. One day, I weighed in and they told me I had gained one pound that week. They jotted it down in my book and I went into the meeting. The leader then asked if anyone had successes that week that they would like to share. I raised my hand and she asked me what my success was. I said, "I only gained one pound this week." So the leader said, "How do you see that as a success?" I said, "Well I was so bad this past week between napping, eating and drinking that I was sure I gained three pounds, so gaining only one pound, to me means I lost two!" I guess I do lie to myself, but I like to call it the power of a positive atti-

Prescription: Laughter

tude. That is still far better than beating yourself up over a pound.

I remember one time going to weigh in and I had been very very good. I was walking three miles a day and swimming 150 laps a week and I was very proud of myself but for three weeks in a row I didn't lose any weight. I went home and I remember just sliding down against the refrigerator in the kitchen, with despair and disappointment overwhelming me and I started to weep. My son Michael was about five at the time. He looked at me and said, "Why are you crying Mommy?" and I said, "because I've been working very hard trying to lose weight and no matter how hard I try, I'm not losing any." He looked at me and said, "Mommy you are the thinniest, most beautifulist, most prettiest mom ever." And my daughter Annie, didn't actually have a cigarette in her mouth, but I could see it in my mind's eye because she pushed him aside and said in the voice of a 45 year divorcee, "Don't lie to her, Michael." And then I laughed till I cried again. I realized how ridiculous this whole thing was. By the way I did go on to lose 30 pounds after that, but don't worry I gained it all back again!

Of course, part of losing weight is exercise, so eventually, I decided I had to put on my big girl pants, and they were big, and join a gym. What I found was that I'm the only one at my gym who needed to be there. Everybody else can go home. They're all thin and fit and showing off by touching their toes. If God wanted me to touch my toes, he would've put them at my knees where I could reach them.

I was in an aerobics class with instructor Lisa. She was very enthusiastic, like a hummingbird on cocaine. She said to me, "Nancy, let's do jumping jacks!" I said, "I'm 68-years-old. If you want me to do jumping jacks you better have a mop." Then a friend of mine asked me if I had ever tried *gentle yoga*. She thought I would love it. I asked, "Have we met?" I was quite sure I would not like gentle yoga, but I tried it. The thing with yoga instructors is that they always sound great. They instruct in a very gentle, soft, calm voice "and now we're doing downward dog." I thought they meant that we'd get on all fours and lift a leg up like a dog at a fire hydrant, but that's not what it is. You bend over at the waist with your hands, reaching for the floor until you find yourself looking like an upside down V. Then she says in that very soothing voice "and now we're all coming up," and I screamed out, "not all of us!" When I got up, I started to walk out of the room to leave, she said, "Nancy, will you be coming back?" I said "I'll come back when you can have a pose I can work on… like Hibernating Bear or Sleeping Cat."

There is a way around joining a gym, though, if you really hate it. Just go out, buy yourself a pair of Spanx, put them on three times fast and that's your cardio for the week! The product gained early attention after being featured on *Oprah's Favorite Things* in November 2000. After it aired, women were like sheep to the slaughter, following the suggestion from Oprah. A pair of Spanx was expensive and I couldn't afford them. Everyone around me said, "Nancy you have to try Spanx. They are fantastic!" Women talking to each other raved about Spanx. I still couldn't afford them.

My niece was getting married and I had a lovely dress that was just the slightest, tiniest bit too tight. I thought to myself this is the time for me to splurge and get my first pair of Spanx. When I was in the hotel room getting ready, I grabbed the Spanx and my dress and went into the bathroom. I opened up the pair of Spanx and the first thing I thought was, *Apparently something has gone very, very wrong with the packaging because they seem to have given me a rubber band.* I went to put them on and the sound coming out of the bathroom alarmed Jack. He said, "What are you doing in there? Lifting weights?" I said, "No, it's much harder than that." I learned you have to put on Spanx in phases. First, you put your legs through them and you hoist the Spanx up over your knees, then stop, have some water and let your heart rate drop until you've recovered. Then go from the knees up over your hips again, safety first, be sure to stay hydrated and take breaks as needed. Then you go from the hips over what I affectionately call "the mountain" and suddenly with a big wallop the Spanx were on. I put my dress on and I was astounded. The dress was actually loose and I never looked thinner.

Now that I'm over 60, I have a superpower and that superpower is that I can hear what people are thinking. When I went to the wedding, all I could hear was, "Look at Nancy doesn't she look fantastic?" then "Wow, Nancy looks terrific." I was strutting around like a peacock. Then… I had to go to the bathroom. Once I got the Spanx down, I didn't have the upper body strength to pull them back up. I didn't know what to do so I took the Spanx off and put them in my pocketbook. When I went back out to the wedding, again with my super-power, I could hear what people were thinking and this time I heard, "Oh my God what happened to Nancy? Did she get pregnant in the bathroom?" Then my sister Carol came running over to me. She said, "What happened to you?" I got a little teary and replied, "Carol I went to the bathroom, and I couldn't put my Spanx back on." Carol whispered to me "Me too. What did you do with your Spanx?" I said, "They're in my purse." Carol then instructed, "Follow me." And I followed her into the fancy-dancy ladies room in the hotel. She went over to the couch that was in the ladies room. She lifted up one of the cushions and there were her Spanx. So I put mine there too, and we went out and enjoyed the rest of the wedding. When the wedding was over she instructed me to get our Spanx. Off I went back to the ladies room. I lifted up the cushion, and there I saw five pairs of Spanx! The next day I signed up for the gym.

Now I'm going to prescribe for you some calorie-free and carb-free jokes!

PRESCRIPTION: Laughter

My doctor told me I was obese. I got defensive and told him, "Look, I'm obese. My sister is obese. My mother is obese. My kids are obese. My brother is obese. Obesity **runs** in my family." The doctor replied, "It sounds like nobody runs in your family."

A married man was having an affair with his secretary. One day, their passions overcame them in the office and they went to her house. Exhausted from the afternoon's activities, they fell asleep and awoke at around 8:00 p.m. As the man threw on his clothes, he told the woman to take his shoes outside and rub them through the grass and dirt. Confused, she nonetheless complied and he slipped into his shoes and drove home. "Where have you been?" demanded his wife when he entered the house. "Darling," replied the man, "I can't lie to you. I've been having an affair with my secretary. I fell asleep in her bed and didn't wake up until eight o'clock." The wife glanced down at his shoes and said, "You liar! You've been playing golf!"

Tiger Woods finished a golf tournament in Waterford, Ireland. He had rented a BMW and stopped at a local gas station to fill it up. When he got out of the car a golf tee fell out of his pocket. The gas attendant picked it up and said, "Now what would this be?" and Tiger Woods said, "It's a golf tee." The gas attendant persisted, "And what would it be used for?" Tiger Woods said, "It holds up my balls when I'm driving," and the gas attendant mused, "Those people from BMW think of everything!"

―――――

A man is on a business trip in Scotland. He had two days to do whatever he wanted after his business deal was done. So he went to Saint Andrews golf course and asked the golf pro if there was anyone that he could play a round of golf with. He wanted a really good golfer. The golf pro said, "Calum MacGregor is the best in these parts and he's right over there." So the businessman goes over to Calum and asks if he could play a round with him the next day. Calum said, "Sure. I would say 10 o'clock. I may be a half hour late, but I'll be there." Then like clockwork he showed up at 10 o'clock the next day and they played a round of golf and the businessman lost. He said to Calum, "That is the best round of golf I've ever played. You are some great player. Can we have a rematch tomorrow?" Calum replied, "Sure, same time 10 o'clock but I might be a half hour late." Calum shows up at 10 o'clock and the businessman noticed that he had left-handed golf clubs

Prescription: Laughter

even though he'd played with right-handed golf clubs the day before. After Calum beat him again the businessman said, "I can't believe yesterday you played with right-handed golf clubs and you were spectacular. Today you had left-handed golf clubs, and you played even better. How do you choose whether you are going to use the right-handed golf clubs or the left-handed ones?" Calum said, "Oh, that's up to me wife. You see if she wakes up on the right side of the bed, I use the right-handed golf clubs. If she wakes up on the left side of the bed, I use the left-handed golf clubs." The businessman said, "Well, what do you do if she wakes up on her back?" Calum answered, "Why then… I'll be a half hour late."

―――

A young man wins a ticket to the Super Bowl. He is absolutely thrilled and he's got spectacular seats. When he gets in his seat, he notices the seat next to him is empty. The one next to the empty seat has an elderly gentleman sitting in it. He thought that perhaps the person in the empty seat was running a little late. But when it was half time, the young man realized no one was coming to sit in that seat, so he said to the elderly gentleman, "Can you believe somebody has tickets to this seat and didn't come?" The elderly gentleman said, "I have season tickets and that seat was my wife's seat. Unfortunately, she passed away." The young man said, "Oh, I'm so sorry but couldn't you find anyone else to take that seat, a friend or relative?" The elderly gentleman looked at him and said, "No… they're all at her funeral."

A man is sitting at a bar listening to two women chatting. He leaned over to them and said, "I'm sorry to interrupt, but I couldn't help noticing the accents you have. Are you two ladies from Scotland?" One of them gave him a scowl and said, "It's Wales, you idiot!" so he said, "Oh I'm so sorry… are you two whales from Scotland?"

Two men are walking through Central Park with their dogs. They get hungry and thirsty and decide to stop in at a nice restaurant for lunch, but they see a sign that says, no dogs allowed. So the first man says to his friend, "Just do what I do." He puts on a pair of sunglasses and goes up to the hostess and says, "I'd like a table." The hostess says, "I'm sorry, sir, no dogs allowed." The man says, "Oh, but you see, this is my seeing eye dog." The hostess says, "Oh! I'm so sorry sir. Of course… come this way" and she takes him to his table. He then looks over at his friend and winks. When the hostess returns, his friend put on his sunglasses and he says to the hostess, "I'd like a table please." And she replied "I'm sorry sir, no dogs allowed." He says, "Oh, but this is my seeing eye dog." The hostess looks at him and says, "Really? They gave you a chihuahua for a seeing eye dog?" He then screams at her, "They gave me a frigging chihuahua?"

Chapter 13
Toddlers & Tiaras Meets Medicare

I've met a lot of queens in my day, it's just that none of them were women! Back in 2019, I was persuaded to participate in the Ms. New York Senior America pageant at age 63. This pageant celebrates women over 60. One of the requirements is to perform a talent for 2 ½ minutes. Some of the contestants had never been on stage, and others were professional performers. The contestants also needed to write and speak about their Philosophy of Life. Finally, they needed to get a dress, find their courage, and throw their sash in the ring! So, off these women went, got their hair done, put on some lipstick, bought a gown, found a talent where they thought there was none, and strutted their stuff in front of a live audience. To their surprise they discovered there was a whole lot more they had to offer the world.

Here is how I got involved with this unique, courageous and simply fabulous group of women. I was doing a show at the Cotuit Theater in Centerville,

Prescription: Laughter

Massachusetts. The next day I got a phone call from the theater, asking if it would be alright if they gave my phone number to a woman who had seen the show the night before, as she wanted to talk to me about a show business opportunity. So I said, "Of course." And then my imagination started going wild. I thought, *Maybe she's a TV executive and wants me to have my own sitcom, or maybe it is a scout from Jimmy Fallon or Jimmy Kimmel.* Shortly after that, my phone rang and I found myself talking to Helen McCarney. She asked if we could meet at her home just a few miles away from The Captain David Kelly House where I was staying. Side note, if you are ever in Cape Cod, in Centerville, do yourself a favor, and stay there. *www.captaindavidkelleyhouse.com*. Once you do, you'll know why I recommended it. I turned to my best friend, confidant and manager, Carol Manire and said, "Should we go meet Helen? I mean… I don't know what this is about but she sounds fun and at the very least, it will be an interesting story."

We got to Helen's house, and it was a beautiful seaside cottage. We walked in and the first thing we saw were crowns and sashes, awards, and trophies everywhere. Helen was gracious, generous, feisty and funny. She said, "I saw you last night and you've got talent and spunk. I think you should audition to become a contestant in the Ms. Senior New York America Pageant." While we sat there, she called her friend Marlene Schuss (before her death in 2023 at age 90) and recommended me for the pagent. Marlene had been the head administrator of Ms. Senior New York America for years along with her partner in love and pageants, Bob Geltman (before his death in 2022 at age 91). Marlene and I talked, and she was as charming a human being as you could ever hope to meet. She could sell milk to a cow! She flattered me and coaxed me by saying that all I had to do was come to an informational meeting for the prospective contestants at a local library, and they were going to have free coffee and doughnuts. Well, she had to know my two favorite things are free coffee and doughnuts! So I went to the meeting and they won me over with their warmth, energy and unique excitement for living life to its fullest. I was all in because Marlene was one in a million and I wanted to be in her world. She encouraged, cajoled, mentored and collaborated with every one of us. She was our personal cheerleader. With Bob by her side and her talented granddaughter, Chiara Klein, as the Director, Marlene put on a great show, and changed so many women's lives for the better.

Marlene Schuss and her granddaughter Chiara Klein

Then in July 2019, the greatest surprise in my life

came when I was crowned Ms. Senior New York America, and also won Miss Congeniality.

A few months later in Atlantic City, I was crowned second runner-up in Ms. Senior America. These events introduced me to this group of women who I never imagined existed. These are women who come together every year and compete, not really against each other, but to see what they themselves are made of. I took a DNA test to see what I was made of, and it came back 90% sugar and 10% Joan Rivers. It was remarkable to see how these women supported each other and made lifelong friendships along the way. It's almost like soldiers in combat, when you go through such scary, harrowing experiences together, you never forget those that were in the trenches with you.

Nancy Witter

The Queens - Eva Mallis Photography

It was so out of my wheelhouse. And though I'm a professional entertainer, it was very scary to go on stage where you're going to be judged, and not by the audience, but by actual judges. Especially since I am not at all competitive. I never played sports. When all my other friends were playing sports, you could usually find me under a shade tree, eating a Devil Dog. I took this on as a challenge and I'm so glad I did.

I had one of the best times in my life in Atlantic City. I had 30 people from all over the country come to cheer me on. I had my sisters, friends, cousins who came to see this unique event. We saw Queens from 1987, or 1991, or 2003, they were all over the place. It reminded me of that scene in Sister Act where all the nuns were running around the casino and the bad guys couldn't find Whoopie Goldberg, because all the nuns were everywhere. One former Queen got around on her motorized Jazzy Mobility Scooter, just like you see in the food stores. They were having a ball scooting around in their sashes and tiaras.

Prescription: Laughter

I'm so glad I said "yes" to Marlene. It taught me a lot. At a certain age it is wise to find something that is out of your comfort zone, something that challenges or even scares you… and then do it anyway. No matter how undeserving you may feel, or how inadequate you think you are… do it anyway! You can always back out if you must, but having the courage to say "YES" will keep life interesting, and your heart beating and ya never know, there could be a crown in your future. One day you're doing dishes, the next… you're looking to buy a crown cleaner!

Pictured below is when I appeared on the Rachel Ray show where they billed my appearance in their press release as:

Senior Pageant Winner Hilariously Throws Herself On The Floor To Demonstrate a Life-Saving Tip.

I couldn't do stand-up comedy for my talent because we only had 2 1/2 minutes. So Carol Manire and I chose to write a song parody to the tune, *If I Could Talk to the Animals* from Doctor Dolittle. We were thinking, *at our age, what we would have told our younger selves?* That is how the song came to be. I can't sing and yet, it has never stopped me! Here are the lyrics to *If I Could Talk To The Younger Me.*

If I could talk to the younger me, just imagine it… chatting with myself at 23
I'd say exercise and moisturize, especially around the eyes, oh God! I hope she listens to me.
If I could have a heart-to-heart with me, when I was 33 I'd advise enthusiastically…
That she be a little frugal, invest heavily in Google and now I'd be living in Capri..
At 43, I'd say, you won't carpool forever and you won't always be a human ATM.
You'll get revenge when Junior goes to college, when you turn his room… into your den.
And if I met me at 53, I'd say honestly… your days of perfect vision are now gone.

Prescription: Laughter

But there's no need to worry, life looks better when it's blurry,
And you won't see that you look just like your mom!
At 63 I can't touch my toes or tie my shoes. My body aches, but my brain feels 22.
When someone asks, can you have fun and feel young again?
I'd say like hell you can... and I do.
So, to conclude, if she had the chance,
I think I know just what my 20 something self would have to say.
She'd say I want your maturity, your Social Security,
Your Medicare, your savoir faire, especially your platinum hair...
And I'd say, oh wait and see, cause you'll be me one day!

Now I'll make you Queen for a day, by prescribing you a big dose of laughter

Nancy Witter

PRESCRIPTION: Laughter

A wife looks at her husband and says "We are so old." He gets very insulted and says to his wife "Maybe you're old, but I'm not." She looked at him and said "Are you kidding me, when you were born the Dead Sea was just sick." He said, "Oh yeah, when you were born, Alexander the Great was just, Alexander the Adequate."

―――

Mom's recipe for iced coffee: Have kids. Make coffee. Forget you made coffee. Put it in the microwave. Forget you put it in the microwave. Open the microwave an hour later and drink iced coffee.

―――

Grandchildren can be so annoying. How many times can you go, 'And the cow goes moo and the pig goes oink?' It's like talking to a supermodel." *Joan Rivers*

―――

A bunch of college girls were graduating and they made a pact to meet every 10 years for their new decade birth-

Prescription: Laughter

days. The first birthday they celebrated together was when they turned 30. One of the girls said "Why don't we go to the Wellington Inn? They have free margaritas on Friday night, and we might meet some men." So they did. Then when they turned 40, another friend said, "You know where we should go? The Wellington Inn because they have free daycare and we can meet each other's children. So they did. Then they turned 50 and one of the women said, "You know where we should go? The Wellington Inn because they put in a new handicap ramp and Karen just had her knees done, and Lisa just had her hips done." And so they did. Then they turned 60. One of the gals said, "You know where we should go? The Wellington Inn. They have a new chef who has a spectacular low sodium menu that I've been dying to try." And so they did. Then they turned 70 and one of the women said, "You know where we should go? The Wellington Inn... Because we've never been there before."

———

There was a widow sitting by the pool at The Villages, in Florida. She looks next to her and finds this very dashing handsome man on a chaise lounge. She said to him, "I've never seen you before. You must be new here." He said, "I am indeed. I just moved in the other day." The woman couldn't help but notice he was very pale so she said to him, "You poor thing, you look like you haven't seen the sun in years." He said, "To be honest I just got out of prison. I was there for 25 years."

The woman said "Oh my goodness, what did you do?" He said, "I killed my wife." To which the woman replied very enthusiastically, "So then… you're single?"

An old man calls his son and says, "Listen, your mother and I are getting a divorce. Forty-five years of misery is more than enough for anyone." "Wait, Dad, what are you talking about?" the son yells, completely shocked. "We just can't stand each other anymore," the old man says, his voice firm. "I'm tired of looking at her, and I don't want to discuss it. Call your sister and break the news to her," and he hangs up. The son, now in a panic, immediately calls his sister. She explodes, "Like heck they are!" She calls their father right back. "You are NOT getting divorced! Don't you dare do a single thing. We are both flying home first thing tomorrow to sort this out. Do not call a lawyer. Do not file a single paper. DO YOU HEAR ME?" She slams the phone down. The old man hangs up, turns to his wife, and says, "Okay, they're both coming for Christmas and paying their own airfares."

A Boy Scout and two other passengers were flying in a small plane at 5000 feet when the pilot came out of the cockpit in a panic. Pilot: "The plane is going to crash! I'm sorry, but we only have three parachutes. I have four young children who need me, so I'm taking one of the parachutes. Good luck figuring out which of the three of you get the other two parachutes." The Scout says, "You guys go ahead, it will be my good turn for the day, to sacrifice my life." One of the other passengers says "Sure, kid. I'm way smarter than anyone, a genius in fact, so the most important thing is that I live." He straps on and jumps out of the plane. The last passenger said, "Kid, I've lived a full life and you have your whole life before you, so, seriously, you should take the last parachute." The Scout then says, "That's OK, sir, we'll both be safe. That genius took my backpack!"

―――

A wife, pissed off that her husband was late again, wrote a dramatic note. "I've had enough. I'm leaving you. Don't try to find me." She hid under the bed, waiting to see his reaction. The husband walks in, finds the note, and after a pause… he scribbles something down, then calls someone. "She's finally gone… yeah, I know, about damn time. I'm coming over. Wear that French nightie I bought you. I love you." He hangs up, grabs his keys, and leaves. The wife, shaking with rage and tears, crawls out from under the bed to read what he wrote. It read: "I can see your feet. Also, we're out of bread. Back in five."

Chapter 14

I'm Not Dead Yet...
But I'm Getting Closer

My best comedy buddy was Ted McElroy. He was incredibly funny and a very talented man. I would always introduce him as the *inappropriate* Ted McElroy. He was truly a comic's comic because he could possibly offend everybody else in the audience, but not the comics. We also knew his heart was so big, and everyone in the audience always took his jokes in the spirit with which they were intended. He was authentic and kind, smart, honest and very funny.

When I met him, he was in his early 50s. We had done a show, and then my friend Ron, Ted and I were sitting around having a great time at Don Giovanni's on 44th Street. We were having so much fun that I missed one train after another until finally, it was 3:45 in the morning and my next train home would be at 5:30 a.m.. Ted said, "Why don't you come stay at my house?" I looked at Ron and he looked at me and we thought, *Poor Ted must live in a dumpy five-story walk up somewhere*, but we agreed to go to his house because we had nowhere else

Prescription: Laughter

to go. To our great surprise, he lived in a beautiful subsidized luxury building two blocks away. We were shocked how beautiful the building was. He took us up to the 14th floor, and when we walked in the first thing we noticed was a beautiful outdoor balcony overlooking the Hudson River, but the furniture in the place was all lawn furniture. As we looked around, I declared, "Ted this is our new Club House." And it was!

When Ted's great friend and neighbor died, he got her furniture. Then a friend of ours moved to London and Ted inherited even more furniture and even a keyboard which came in handy for the after shows at The Club House. Those were the best years of my life, and I never laughed so hard. Ted smoked a lot, drank a lot and was a huge pothead. It made for a fun friend, but in terrible health.

One of his signature stories was that he had his gallbladder taken out. During the course of the operation, they nicked his spleen and unbeknownst to Ted he was bleeding internally, but he told the story like this:

"I was sitting with a few of my friends in the apartment and I knew something was wrong. It was hard to breathe and I was getting weak. My friends said I looked pale and gray and I should go to the hospital. I said to them, 'You know what… I'll just smoke a little bit of my bong and that'll make me feel better.' So I lit up the bong and I couldn't draw enough breath to light my bong… I called 911 faster than a dog running after a meat truck. The operator said, 'What is the nature of your emergency?' and I said, 'I can't light my bong!' and she said, 'Sir, even in New York City that's not considered an emergency!' I said, 'No, you don't understand, I can't draw enough breath to light my bong.' So they sent an ambulance over and as I'm in the ambulance the EMT tending to me said, 'We're gonna go to Saint Charles Hospital.' And I said 'No please that's a terrible hospital, people check in and they never *check* out. Take me to Mount Sinai,' and he said, 'that's six blocks away sir, you may not make it.' And all I could think was, *I only have six blocks to live? My last sights on this earth are going to be seeing a homeless man pee on the sidewalk, a prostitute propositioning a Priest, and a rat scurrying across the street.* I said, 'Okay St. Charles is fine, I'm going to miss too much if I check out now.'

"When I was in the hospital they discovered I had a blood disease, and they told me I only have 10 to 12 years to live. I was so bummed out, I thought, *What can I do with that?* Nothing. I mean if I was given 3 to 6 months I could do something fun. I could rob a bank, I could do all the drugs I've always wanted to try, eat and drink as much as I want, which actually I did anyway! But 10-12 years, it's just so random, not even worth telling anyone.

"Now at that time, I was looking for a new mattress and I was talking to the mattress salesman and I said, 'Why is this mattress $1,000 and that mattress (pointing to another) $1,500? What is the difference?' The manager said, 'Well, the $1,000 one comes with a 10 year warranty and the $1,500 one comes with a 15 year warranty.' I said 'I've just been given 10 to 12 years to live, so I'm not sure which one to choose.' The salesman said, 'No one has ever said that to me before.' Ted replied, 'I think I'll take the one with the 10 year warranty and take my chances on having a bad back for the next three.'"

Another time Ted was in the hospital on a ventilator (before the pandemic). I said to him "Ted, if you make it out of this hospital alive, you're gonna do a one-man show and I'm going to produce it." He did make it out of the hospital and I produced the show and it was called "Ted McElroy in… *I'm Not Dead Yet*."

I hosted the show and I introduced Ted by saying "Ted has recovered after spending three weeks in ICU last month. He has made it out and he's here with us tonight. Just so you all know, no one deserved to be in ICU, more than Ted. He worked hard his whole life to get there. He hasn't eaten a vegetable in years, when the doctor said take your medicine with a clear liquid, he assumed he meant vodka. He has smoked cigarettes for 50 years and weed for 40 years, so Ted, you are a walking miracle and we're so glad… you're not dead yet!" It was a huge hit and a year later we did another one man show for Ted and we called that one *I'm not dead yet… But I'm getting closer*. Again, it was a very successful show.

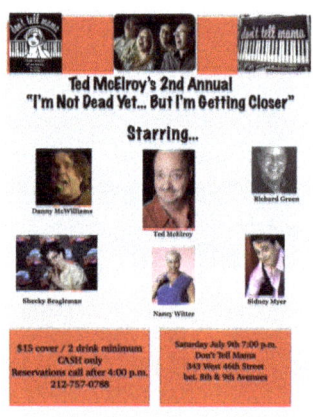

Six months after this show, my Ted died. He was cremated and we had his memorial service in the showroom at Don't Tell Mama, where we had his two sold out solo shows. We made a flyer for the funeral and it said, I'm Not Dead Yet, but with the words '*not*' and '*yet*' crossed out. It was sold out. People got up and told stories of being in shows with Ted, his best jokes, and other ways that Ted impacted their life. It was an evening of pure love, joy and laughter. Once again proving life can be tragic, and funerals can be fun. What a way to go!

Prescription: Laughter

In my tribute to Ted that night, I told a story of this one particular night. My daughter, Annie, had come to our Saturday night show with her friend Ryan and his mother and his mother's friend. After the show, we were talking with them outside the club and Ted invited them back to The Club House. Every Saturday night after the show, the comedians would go back, sometimes with people from the audience or sometimes people we met in the elevator! I imagine Saturday nights at The Club House must have been like the Saturday Night Live after-party, except I think we probably had more fun. So Annie and her group came back to The Club House and we literally had an after show with about 25 people. We took turns telling stories, telling jokes, with our songwriter friends playing songs on the keyboard he inherited.

Ted went over and introduced himself to Annie's entourage. He said to the mother of Annie's friend Ryan, "Oh, your son Ryan is so handsome. Do you have any more like him at home?" and the mother said, "I did Ted, but he overdosed and died and this is the first time I have been out in a year." Ted looked at her and said, "Oh my God, I am so sorry. What are you drinking?" She said, "a gin and tonic." Ted replied, "we're gonna have to put more gin in that drink," and he did. The party went on until two or three in the morning. Ryan's mom and her friend finally headed to the door. Ted and I said goodbye, as they were the last to go. We all hugged and kissed as if we were old friends. Ryan's mom looked up at Ted and said, "Ted, I want to thank you for giving me the best night in my worst year. I literally never thought I would ever laugh again. This is the first time since Luke died that I believe I might survive. I feel hopeful and I never thought I would feel that either, so, thank you."

It illustrates the healing power of laughter. It will never cure permanent heartbreak, but it can give you a respite from it, and that can make all the difference. I was always proud of my friend Ted, but never more than that night.

Now for your prescription for laughter... I prescribe some of Ted's favorite jokes. They will cure what ails you!

PRESCRIPTION: Laughter

People say that gay marriage is tearing away at our social fabric. Do you really believe gays would do anything to harm fabric? *David Hodorowski*

———

A prostitute goes up to this unsuspecting man and whispers in his ear, "I'll do whatever you want for 50 bucks." He says, "Great! Paint my house!" Henny Youngman

———

Peter Marshall: When Richard Nixon was Vice President, he went someplace on a "good will mission," but instead wound up being stoned and shouted at. Where did this take place?
Paul Lynde: Pat Nixon's bedroom.

———

Peter Marshall: Paul, why do Hell's Angels wear leather?
Paul Lynde: Because chiffon wrinkles too easily.

Peter Marshall: Paul, is there such a thing as a female rooster?

Paul Lynde: Yeah, they're the ones who just go, "a doodle doo!"

———

A man calls the front desk of the hotel where he is staying and Ted answers. He says, "tonight we turn the clocks back an hour. Does that mean I get an extra hour of sleep?" Ted answered, "You get an extra hour, what you choose to do with it is totally up to you. Personally, I wouldn't waste it sleeping." Ted McElroy

———

A man and a woman were sitting beside each other in the first class section of the plane. The woman sneezed, took out a tissue, gently wiped her nose and then shuddered quite violently for 10 or 15 seconds. The man went back to his reading. A few minutes later, the woman sneezed again, took a tissue, gently wiped her nose and shuddered quite violently as before. The man was becoming more and more curious about the shuddering. A few more minutes passed and the woman sneezed one more time. Again she took a tissue, gently wiped her nose and shuddered violently. The man couldn't restrain his curiosity any longer. He turned to the woman, and said, "You've sneezed three times,

Prescription: Laughter

wiped your nose with a tissue, then shuddered violently! Are you all right?" "I'm sorry if I disturbed you," the woman replied, "I have a rare condition. You see, every time I sneeze, I have an orgasm." The man was a little embarrassed but even more curious and said, "I've never heard of that before. What are you taking for it?" The woman looked at him and said, "Pepper."

———

There was this couple who had been married for 20 years. Every time they made love the husband always insisted on turning off the lights. Well, after 20 years the wife felt this was ridiculous. She figured that she would break him out of this crazy habit. So one night, while they were in the middle of a wild, screaming, romantic session, she turned on the lights. She looked down... and saw her husband was holding a battery-operated pleasure device... a vibrator! She went completely ballistic. "You impotent idiot," she screamed at him, "how could you be lying to me all of these years? You better explain yourself!" The husband looks her straight in the eye, and says calmly, "I'll explain the toy... You explain the kids."

Chapter 15

McDougal Motto: It Could Always be Worse

My father and mother both taught me that when something happens, it could be tragic, sad or unfortunate, but there is more than one way to look at it and process it. The thing that makes the difference, of course, is your point of view and your attitude which is true of almost anything in life. They both hated bad news, and could turn terrible into terrific, in a heartbeat. I inherited my optimism from them both and it has never failed me.

I lived in San Antonio for a year right after I got married. When we moved back to New York, I went to dinner with my dad and in the course of the evening, I said to him, "So, how's Grandma?" You know, a little small talk and catching up. Without skipping a beat he said, "Oh, she died." I said "SHE DIED? Why didn't you tell me?" and he said, "Well you weren't gonna fly all the way back from San Antonio to go to her funeral, so why would I call you with news you couldn't do anything about?" Then I said, "Because she was my grandmother, she wasn't a goldfish." Then he said "Well, it's not like she noticed you weren't there." And so then I just ordered another glass of wine.

It's not the first time something like that happened in my family. My Aunt Nancy used to have Easter at her house every year. And it was a big crowd, probably 35 to 40 people and those were just her brothers and sisters and their children. One year my brother Steven was chatting with my Aunt Virginia and asked, "Where's Uncle Harry?" Aunt Virginia replied, "Oh Steven, Uncle Harry died about six months ago." And Steven shouted, "Nobody in my family tells me anything. Why didn't you guys tell me Uncle Harry died?" I think the answer was, I thought Ditta told him, Carol thought I told him, Paul thought my dad told him. Now… if somebody even gets an ingrown toenail the first thing we do is call Steven to let him know.

A great example of my father's positive spirit and optimism happened almost 30 years ago. My stepbrother Tommy O'Connor was locked out of his apartment in New York City and climbed up a fire escape to try to go in through the window and he slipped and fell five stories. I got a phone call in the morning and it was my brother Paul telling me this news. I asked him for details but he didn't have any. I was on my way to get my haircut and had to drive by my father's house so I stopped in. I saw my father and said, "Dad, I just heard about Tommy. Is he OK?" And my father said, "He's great." I said, "He's great?" and he said "Fantastic." So I said to my father, "I have to get my haircut but when I'm done, I'm coming back 'cause I wanna hear all about it." I was leaving the hair salon and ran into my friend Jean Gallic. She was a nurse at the same hospital Tommy was admitted to, and she said to me, "Did you hear about Tommy? You know, I'm his nurse at the hospital." I said, "Oh I'm so glad he was in such good hands. When did he get released?" she said "Released? Released??? Nancy, he broke almost every bone in his body. He didn't hit his head or break his back but he's in traction and is going to be in the hospital for weeks. Then, he'll be in rehab for months." So of course I looked at her and said, "Oh yeah, no... no... no... I knew that. Thanks for confirming."

I then raced back to my father's house. I saw him at the kitchen table and actually screamed, "What is wrong with you? I asked you how Tommy was and you told me he was great, as a matter of fact, you said, fantastic. I just ran into his nurse and she told me that he's gonna be in the hospital for weeks and rehab for months." Then my father, who rarely raised his voice to me, got in my face and yelled, "You listen to me, by all rights today we should be at Tommy's funeral. Next to death... I think he's doing great... fantastic! He's going to recover and one day it will be like this never happened."

I tell this story to illustrate that there are different ways to interpret and process the same event. I wasn't wrong. This was a catastrophic injury, and I had every right to be concerned and upset to see it as the terrible accident it was. Now my father wasn't wrong either. He had the advantage of age and experience to know as bad as this was, it could have been much worse and we should be grateful that it was something Tommy could

Prescription: Laughter

recover from. He chose to process it from the most positive point of view possible. Just so you know, Tommy made a full recovery. He went on to be the most successful person in our blended family. He has two children and has lived a very happy life.

Over the years I've had friends who had cancer or been injured and had a long recovery ahead of them. The very first thing I say is "Let's start at the end, you're going to be fine. It's just that between now and fine, you're going to have to go over a very big mountain, but luckily you have sherpas in the form of friends that will get you there." I'm very happy that everyone I ever said that to did indeed survive and thrive.

My mother was also a very positive person. She was at a party soon after she was diagnosed with cancer and this was in 1972, when it was barely spoken about. An acquaintance at the party said to her, "Dolores I'm so sorry to hear that you are sick." My mother jokingly said, "It's nothing really, just a touch of cancer."

One of my favorite stories that highlights my mother's spirit was what I call the "Monkey Story." My father was voted in as President of Richmond Hill Savings Bank in 1970. My mother could not have been more excited. She was now the wife of a bank President. I think she ran out and bought a pill box hat and a pink Chanel suit as soon as she heard the news.

She thought she was now the Lady of the house and wanted to show off her hostess skills. So she decided to have a very fancy formal dinner party at our home, and invite the Board of Directors and their wives. She made beef wellington, twice baked potatoes, spinach soufflé, and Caesar salad. She cleaned and fussed and polished silver and brought out the good china and crystal. She was born for this. Everything was perfect.

My brother Walter loved animals, and acquired a variety of them. One day he came home with a pet monkey named Charlie. He was a small spider monkey with a long tail and we adored him, as much as my parents hated him. That particular night all my brothers and sisters were out, and I was home so I was the hired help, without the pay. My job was to help serve and then clear the table. I loved cooking and being in the kitchen with my mother. It was such a great night. The ladies wore their beautiful dresses, had their hair done and the men were in their beautiful suits and ties. After dinner was served, I got a little bored just waiting around to clear the table. So, I went down to the basement and brought Charlie up to the kitchen in his crate to keep me company.

Our kitchen had full length shuttered swinging doors dividing the kitchen from the formal dining room. I took Charlie out of his cage and was playing with him at the kitchen table near the door. Suddenly, with no warning my mother backed into the kitchen and as the doors burst open, it startled Charlie and he sprang out of my arms onto the door and then swung into the dining room, landing on top of the chandelier. Uh Oh! Oops! My mother looked at me, frozen in the kitchen eyeing the silver platter with the remains of the beef wellington on it. She said very, very, very, calmly with her eyes closed "Please Nancy... pleeeeaazzzzz! Tell me that stupid monkey is not in our dining room." My heart sank, and I said, "Don't worry Mom, I'll get him." I ran into the dining room and tried to reassure everybody that everything was fine. These people were totally horrified, my mother mortified and my father could have committed homicide! I brought in the cut up apple that I had been feeding Charlie, lifted a piece up to him and whispered, "come on Charlie, come on down." The plan was when he reached up for the apple I would grab him by his stupid tiny monkey arms. Charlie snatched the piece of apple out of my hands and proceeded to eat the mealy part and spit out the uneaten skin which landed onto the top of the huge bouffant hairdo (it was the 70's) of one of the wives.

Now my mother regained her composure and quickly ushered the women out of the dining room into the living room and she whipped up the biggest batch of martinis she could muster. By now, the men were strategizing as to how to capture the beast. I heard one of them say, "What we need is a banana!" They all thought they were on *Mutual of Omaha's Wild Kingdom*. They felt like hunters after the big game, please… it was a one-pound monkey!

Nancy Witter

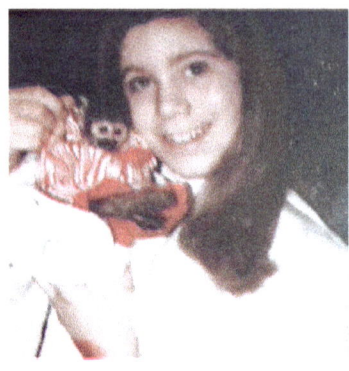

My mother was plying these women with as much alcohol as she could. She later said that her plan was that they would get so drunk that the next morning when they woke up, they would say, "I had the oddest dream last night. I dreamt that the McDougal's had a monkey on the loose in their dining room."

My mother continued to distract these women, but soon she just gave up and after several martinis she said to them, "I'm so sorry for this big mess. I worked so hard to try to have such a nice dinner party and impress you all, and it was ruined by a monkey. I hate that monkey, I hate those kids and Bub drives me crazy!" Then one of the women in an attempt to comfort my mother said, "You think that's bad, my son likes to wear my underwear." Then another said "I don't know what I'm going to do. My daughter's three months pregnant and the wedding is three months away." Little by little these women opened up to each other as the façade behind their big hairdos, fancy dresses and sparkly jewelry crumbled. In that debris, they found comfort in each other, with the help of alcohol and a monkey. It seemed to me to be like, "I'll show you mine.. if you show me yours." You see once you are secure, honest and brave enough to allow people to see your imperfections, and fallibilities, it allows them to share theirs as well.

In the meantime in the dining room, the men had taken their jackets and ties off, they were trying to trick Charlie, so they gave him bananas, grapes and apples. They got the crate and cordoned off the dining room to keep him contained. No good. He left and swung into the drapes. Now the women are totally bombed and coaching and encouraging their husbands. The men were drinking straight scotch as they spent hours trying to get that cagey monkey.

Suddenly the front door opens, and in comes my brother Walter. He was always like Doctor Doolittle. He sees Charlie, whistles, and Charlie swings right onto Walter's shoulder and off they walk. Game over.

Now everyone congratulated each other on a job well done and laughed about it for the rest of the night. They had all been in battle together, they felt a camaraderie they never otherwise would have known.

Because it ultimately ended up as a very successful night, my mother forgave me. While we were in the kitchen chatting about the night, I noticed one of her false eyelashes was missing so I said "Mom you're missing one of your eyelashes." She said "I know." So I said, "Well the next time that happens you should take the other fake eyelash off and that way at least you'll match." She said, "Nancy, I would never do that because the people looking at me on the side with the false eyelash… will still think I look fantastic."

My mother said that it was not the dinner party she envisioned or wanted, yet it was her greatest triumph as a hostess. She saw these women frequently at banking dinners and conferences and remained great friends with this group for the rest of her short life. I still have nightmares about it.

Now stop monkeying around, and take your prescription for laughter!

Prescription: Laughter

PRESCRIPTION: Laughter

A man is driving down the road and comes to a stop sign. He slows down, looks both ways, and since no cars are coming he drives through the intersection. The next thing he knows he's getting pulled over by the police. The policeman comes over to the driver's side of the car and says, "Sir, I pulled you over because you went through that stop sign without stopping." The man is quite indignant and says to the police officer, "I saw the stop sign, I slowed down, I looked both ways, and no cars were coming, so I proceeded." The officer said "Yes sir, but you did not stop." The man said, "I slowed down, slowing down and stopping are the same thing." The officer said, "It's not the same," and to prove it, he took out his billie club and started to hit the man over the head and said, "Now do you want me to stop, or do you want me to slow down?"

―――

An Irish priest is driving down to New York and gets stopped for speeding in Connecticut. The state trooper smells alcohol on the priest's breath and then sees an empty wine bottle on the floor of the car. He says, "Sir, have you been drinking?" "Just water," says the priest.

The trooper says, "Then why do I smell wine?" The priest looks at the bottle and says, "Good Lord! He's done it again!"

———

A gentleman goes up to a woman at a bar and says, "May I buy you a cocktail?" She replied, "No thank you. All alcohol is bad for my legs." The man said, "Sorry to hear that. Do they swell?" She replied "No, they separate."

———

A man is trapped on his roof during a flood and prays to God for help. A rowboat comes by, but the man refuses help, saying he's praying to God and believes God will save him. A motorboat then arrives, and the man gives the same response, stating he has faith. Finally, a helicopter appears, offering him a ride to safety. The man again declines, relying on his faith that God will save him. The water rises, and the man drowns and goes to Heaven. He asks God why He didn't save him despite his faith. God replies, "You idiot! I sent you a rowboat and a motorboat and a helicopter—what more did you want?"

———

A highway patrolman pulled alongside a speeding car on the freeway. Glancing at the car, he was astounded to

Prescription: Laughter

see that the blonde behind the wheel was knitting! Realizing that she was oblivious to his flashing lights and siren, the trooper cranked down his window, turned on his bullhorn and yelled, "PULL OVER!" "NO!" the blonde yelled back, "Turtleneck!"

———

A successful rancher died and left everything to his devoted wife. She was a very good-looking woman and was determined to keep the ranch. Sadly, she knew very little about ranching, so she decided to place an ad in the newspaper for a ranch hand. She hired the first one she interviewed. For weeks, the two of them worked, and the ranch was doing very well. Then one day, the rancher's widow said to the hired hand, "You have done a really good job, and the ranch looks great. You should go into town and kick up your heels." The hired hand readily agreed and went into town one Saturday night. He returned around 2:30 a.m. in the morning, and upon entering the room, he found the rancher's widow sitting by the fireplace with a glass of wine, waiting for him. She quietly called him over to her. "Unbutton my blouse and take it off," she said. Trembling, he did as she directed. "Now take off my boots." He did as she asked, ever so slowly. "Now take off my socks." He removed each gently and placed them neatly by her boots. "Now take off my skirt." He slowly unbuttoned it, constantly watching her eyes in the fire light. "Now take off my bra." Again, with trembling hands, he did as he was told and dropped it to the floor. "Now," she said, "take off my panties." By the light of the fire, he slowly pulled them down and off. Then she looked at him and said, "If you ever wear my clothes into town again, you're fired."

———

A man is speeding on the highway at 2:00 a.m.. A police officer pulls him over and says "Hello sir, I clocked you doing 75 in a 60 mile an hour zone. Is there any reason you were going so fast?" He said "Yes officer, I'm on my way to hear a lecture on the perils of alcohol abuse." The officer said "Who is giving a lecture at 2:00 in the morning?" He said, "My wife."

Chapter 16

Oh Brother!

I have always told my children, and reminded my clients, that life is effort. Sometimes to find that rainbow, you really have to crane your neck. I mean, if you look at something straight on, it can look hopeless and even tragic, but if you tilt your head sideways, close one eye, and blink, you'll think hmmm … if I look at it like that, it isn't so bad.

Remember for every action there is a reaction. You may not have any control over the action, but you always have control over the reaction. Those clichés are clichés for a reason, because they're true. You reap what you sow, the more you give, the more you get and many more.

This was illustrated within my own family. I have three brothers. On December 28, 2013, we lost my brother Walter McDougal when he was hit by a drunk driver. He was already a widower, so that made my niece an orphan. The story of course is tragic. We couldn't change the tragedy, but we could certainly change the outcome.

My brother Walter was a unique and lovable guy. He was born with a birth-related brain injury from lack of oxygen (hypoxic-ischemic encephalopathy). Though he went to a special school, he was a bright and capable adult, had a great sense of humor and a huge capacity for love. He did have issues with impulse control and other challenges, but his charm got him out of a lot of jams. He had a full-time job in a chemical plant, never missed a day of work, except for a few days for his wife's funeral. He was such a dedicated employee.

He joined the army when he was 18. When we asked him why, he said, "it's too crowded here." Well then, good luck in a platoon. When he got back from Boot Camp, we asked him how he liked the Army. He said "I love it! Do you know that when you go missing they notice… and unlike Mom, they come looking for you!" He went to Vietnam, came home and got married. He and his wife Cindy tried for years to have a baby and had eventually accepted the fact that it was not meant to be. Then after 10 years of marriage, they were blessed with a baby girl… Shannon Abigail McDougal on August 15, 2000. It was the biggest surprise of their lives, and the best thing that ever happened to them.

Prescription: Laughter

Cindy, Shannon & Walter

He and Cindy loved this little miracle. Tragedy struck when quite suddenly Cindy passed away. Walter was ill-equipped to be a single father of an eight-year-old girl. So as a family, we got together and my brother Paul and his wife, Adrienne, offered to have Shannon come live with them. We decided that would be the best case scenario for Shannon. They have three other children a little older than Shannon, so she found herself going from an only child to being the baby sister of Liz, Kathryn and Kevin.

Liz, Kathryn, Kevin, Shannon

After Cindy died, Walter sold their home, and relocated closer to his job. He had no car which meant he had to take several trains, and travel an hour or more to my brother Paul's house to see Shannon. He made that long commute so he wouldn't miss a game, a Christmas concert, dance recital or any other event. He always showed up. Sometimes if it was in the evening, he didn't get home until after 11:00 p.m. and had to be at work at 6:00 a.m.. Very often my brother Steven would drive him home when he was able. He helped Walter and Shannon often, and in any way he could. My brother Steven is like that.

Paul, Steven, Walter, Shannon

The most remarkable thing about Walter was throughout all of this, I never once heard him complain. He lived in an area with a very high crime rate. When we cautioned him about this, he said, "I was in Vietnam, I'm used to the sound of gunshots." When he first looked at his apartment, he saw a bullet hole and said to his landlord, "Is that a bullet hole?" and the landlord said, "Yes, but don't worry about it. It was *outgoing*." One time he said to us, "I was walking home and boy, it was busy in the neighborhood last night.

Prescription: Laughter

Now I know how Custer felt." He was always a very optimistic guy. Another time when he got himself in a jam and wrote to my parents. He said, "I just want you to know, I got into a little trouble, so I have some good news and bad news. The bad news is they put me in solitary confinement. The good news is, I finally got my own room!"

Walter and Adrienne

My brother Paul and his wife, Adrienne, are the real heroes of this story. They loved and guided Shannon. As soon as Shannon was old enough, she volunteered at Camp Anchor, an acronym for **A**nswering the **N**eeds of **C**itizens with **H**andicaps through **O**rganized **R**ecreation (ANCHOR) in Lido Beach, NY. All the McDougal kids volunteered there every summer so Shannon had great role models, and the bar was set very high. She spent several years there and has dedicated her short life to helping those with physical, mental and emotional disabilities. I'm proud to say, she graduated from the College of Holy Cross and is now working on her graduate degree in Speech Pathology at SUNY New Paltz, New York.

Paul, Shannon, Adrienne at Shannon's college graduation

Finding the rainbow in this story wasn't easy, but it was there. Walter's death was tragic, but in the debris of this tragedy, we discovered what we were truly made of. Our love for family was tested, and I couldn't love or be more proud of our dysfunctional, imperfect family.

Now to lift your spirits, take your prescription for laughter!

Shannon & Walter

PRESCRIPTION: Laughter

The 8th grade science teacher, Mrs. Parks, asked her class, "Which human body part increases to ten times its size when stimulated?" No one answered, until little Mary stood up angrily and said, "You should not be asking 8th graders a question like that! I'm going to tell my parents, and they will go and tell the principal, who will then fire you!" With a sneer on her face, she then sat back down. Mrs. Parks ignored her and asked the question again: "Which body part increases to 10 times its size when stimulated?" Little Mary's mouth fell open. She said to those around her, "Boy, is she going to get in big trouble!" The teacher continued to ignore her and asked the class, "Anybody?" Finally, Billy stood up, looked around nervously, and replied, "The body part that increases 10 times its size when stimulated is the pupil of the eye." "Very good, Billy," said Mrs. Parks. Then, turning to Mary, she said: "As for you, young lady, I have three things to say. One, you have a dirty mind. Two, you didn't read your homework. And three, one day you are going to be very, very disappointed."

A man is driving down a deserted stretch of highway when he notices a sign out of the corner of his eye. It reads: SISTERS OF ST. FRANCIS HOUSE OF PROSTITUTION 10 MILES. He thinks this is a figment of his imagination and drives on without second thought. Soon he sees another sign which reads: SISTERS OF ST. FRANCIS, HOUSE OF PROSTITUTION, NEXT RIGHT. His curiosity gets the best of him and he pulls into the driveway. He goes up and rings the bell. The door is answered by a nun who asks, "What may we do for you my son?" He answers, "I saw your signs along the highway and was interested in. . . um . . . possibly doing business...." She then said, "Very well my son, follow the winding hallway to the end." He finds himself at the end of a very long hallway and sees a door that says "Knock here." When he did, another nun, in a long habit and holding a tin cup, said to him, "Please place $100 in the cup then go through the next door." He puts $100 in the cup and goes through the next door. It then slams shut behind him and locks. He then finds himself back in the parking lot facing another sign:

GO IN PEACE. YOU HAVE JUST BEEN SCREWED BY THE SISTERS OF ST. FRANCIS.

———

An Irishman walks out of a pub… …It could happen!

———

Prescription: Laughter

Murphy texts his wife which reads, "I'm with the Lads having one last pint. I'll be home in a half hour. If I'm not… read this text again!"

———

In a convent in county Clare, Mother Superior called all the nuns together and said to them, "Sisters, we found that the convent has acquired a case of gonorrhea." Sister Antonio Maria said, "Thank God, I was getting so tired of the chardonnay."

———

Mary O'Connor meets up with her local priest and says, "Oh, Father, I've got some horrible news. My husband passed away last night." The priest says, "Oh, that's terrible. Now tell me, Mary, did he have any last requests?" She says, "That he did, Father." The priest says, "What did he ask, Mary?" She said, "He looked at me Father, and said, 'Mary, for the love of God, put down the gun…'"

———

Muldoon lived alone in the Irish countryside outside of Dublin with only a pet dog for company. One day the dog died, and Muldoon went to the parish priest and asked, "Father, my dog is dead. Could ya' be saying' a Mass for the poor creature?" Father Patrick replied, "I'm afraid not. We cannot have services for an animal in the church. But there are some Baptists down the lane, and there's no tellin' what they believe. Maybe they'll do something for the creature." Muldoon said, "I'll go right away Father. By the way Father, do ya' think $5,000 is enough to donate to them for the service?" Father Patrick exclaimed, "Sweet Mary, Mother of Jesus! Why didn't ya tell me the dog was Catholic?"

Man dies in a beer vat accident. The boss goes to his house to tell his wife. He says to her, "It was terrible, Fiona. He fell into a vat of Guinness Stout and drowned." "Oh my dear God! But you must tell me, Tim. Did he at least go quickly?" "Well, Fiona I'm afraid not. In fact, he got out three times to pee."

A man is reading his newspaper and says to his wife, "Oh my God, it says here, our neighbor Joe, is the local barber and just got arrested for being a drug dealer. Hmmm… I had no idea he was a barber."

Epilogue

I hope this book illustrates that, though your circumstances may be out of your control, your perspective and attitude are not. They are your superpowers. When things are at their worst, that's when comedy is at its best. That's what it is there for, it's the remedy, the antidote.

Just when you think you know where your life is going and how your story will end, something unexpected and surprising can come along and change everything. I always believe everything is going to work out, not that it always does, but when it doesn't I'm shocked. When what I wanted gets cancelled or lost it is almost always replaced with something even better. That is what I like to call a happy mistake.

Life is always unpredictable, you never know what surprises are in your future. I never thought I'd ever remarry after being single for 20 years, and I never thought I'd move from New York to North Carolina.

Both were the biggest surprises of my life. I often think of the randomness that made some people stars. Ed Sullivan started as a sports reporter and eventually took over the Broadway column for the New York Daily News. In 1948, Sullivan was hired by CBS to host Toast of the Town. They thought he was awful, but they kept him on and they later renamed it The Ed Sullivan Show. He never saw that coming either.

Pamela Anderson wasn't discovered in Hollywood. She was discovered on the Jumbotron at a Canadian football game. One minute she's drinking a beer in the stands, the next she's the face of Labatts Beer, then on the cover of Playboy, and then running in slow motion on Baywatch. It is proof that sometimes all it takes to become a star is a good seat at the game and a really flattering camera angle.

Harrison Ford, while working as a carpenter on the Star Wars set, was asked to read lines for actors auditioning for *Star Wars*. George Lucas, who had previously cast him in *American Graffiti*, recognized Ford's natural charisma and humor during the readings and decided to cast him as Hans Solo.

My father had been a widower for years, when he met, and then married Phyllis O'Connor who was the mother of 9. I don't think my father ever thought he would get remarried, and he certainly didn't think he would be not only the father of 7, but the stepfather of 9, making us a family of 16. I think we set a record even for Garden City. At least we lived in the right town for it! They went on to be happily married for 20 years. The

Prescription: Laughter

McDougal/O'Connor clan was bigger and better than the Brady bunch. I graduated high school with my friend and now stepbrother Billy. Almost everyone in my family had a corresponding sibling with the O'Connor family. I'm so grateful my Dad and Phyllis got together because we all think the more the merrier and that certainly is true in this case. As a bonus, it has been an endless source of material!

This is just a normal get together with O'Connors, McDougals, and their kids

I love stories like this because it gives hope that anything can happen. Just when you think something is impossible… BAM your life has changed!

So if you are going through a heartache, recovering from health challenges, financial difficulties, or gut wrenching disappointments, know that this too will someday be a distant memory. Remember if you can laugh through it, you can get through it.

I tried to show by example, in this little book, how catastrophes can be turned into a comedy. Laugh about the imperfections and catastrophes in your life. I've made a living doing this! Be grateful for all that you have, as humble as it may be, because it could always be worse. Always focus on what you DO have, not what you don't have and what you CAN do, not what you can't do. This small shift can change everything. There is a choice you have on how to process any event in your life…choose wisely.

Though I never became a Nurse Practitioner, look at me now prescribing laughter like it's covered by Medicare Part D. By writing I try to paint pictures with my words, so this is my portrait, and love letter to family and friends.

Laughter doesn't change what happened, but it is what helps you heal. Believe anything is possible and that your best chapters are still unwritten.

This QR code will take you to www.nancywitter.com

where you can see videos of some of the references in this book.

"Nancy Witter on Telling Jokes on the Drums"
    "Growing Up McDougal"
    "We Put The Fun in Funerals"
    "If I Could Talk To The Younger Me"

About the Author

Nancy Witter is an award-winning comedian, author, and motivational speaker known for her signature blend of humor and heart. She is a four-time New York City MAC Award winner for Outstanding Female Comedian, and was a finalist on *Nick at Nite's* Search for the Funniest Mom in America. Nancy toured the country for more than five years with the hit comedy trio *Mama's Night Out*, performing to sold-out theaters nationwide.

In 2019, she was crowned Senior Ms. New York America and later appeared on *The Rachael Ray Show* in a memorable, laugh-filled segment for seniors. Her additional TV credits include Lifetime's *Mom's Cooking* and *NickMom Night Out*.

Nancy received her Professional Certification in Life Coaching from NYU and blended her coaching insight with her stand-up experience to write her first book, *Who's Better Than Me? A Guide to Living Happily Ever After*. Today, she is a sought after comedic motivational speaker, celebrated for empowering audiences with her trademark mix of wit, wisdom and authenticity.

Nancy lives in Wilmington, NC with her husband Jack and their "doghter" Liza Minnelli, and is the proud mom of Annie and Michael and doting grandmother to Ellie and Sam. She continues to perform stand-up and deliver keynotes nationwide. Her motto? "If you can laugh through it, you can get through it."

www.ingramcontent.com/pod-product-compliance
Lightning Source LLC
Chambersburg PA
CBHW061735070526
44585CB00024B/2684